house of doctors

TRIPTI SHARAN

Readomania

Readomania Publishing
A division of Kurious Kind Media Private Limited
466, DDA SFS Apartments, Pocket 1, Sector 22, Dwarka,
New Delhi – 110077
books.readomania.com
email: support@readomania.com
Facebook: facebook.com/iamreadomania
Twitter: twitter.com/iamreadomania

First Published in 2018 by Readomania

This book is based on true events. However, instances and characters have been fictionalised.

ISBN: 978-93-858541-2-5

Typeset in Palatino Linotype by Shine Graphics
Printed in India by Thomson Press India Ltd.

Readomania

India has traditionally been the land of storytellers and a lot of us have an inherent skill of creating good plots, good stories and good narrations. With a little encouragement and support, many more authors will be widely read and attain a place in the sun. This is the essence of *Readomania*—an initiative that nurtures emerging stars of the literary world.

It would not be an exaggeration to say that *Readomania* is the talent hunt in fiction. It goes a step beyond by not just identifying the talent but also nurturing it and showcasing it to the world. In the process, we have created a powerhouse of content.

Readomania has four principle interest areas—traditional print publishing, online library of short stories and poetry, literary events and products.

The print publishing works towards delivering good quality content to the readers. We publish good authors in meaningful anthologies, novels and works of narrative non-fiction. Our books stand out for their perspectives, the plots, the language and most importantly their ability to enrich lives.

Take a break, read something nice, write something beautiful. Read our books or visit us at www.readomania.com and enjoy a whole new world of literature.

To my husband, Dhiren,

To my soul sister, Keerti

&

To all those who dare to undergo the drill

To give us hope and healing;

The 'angels' in white,

We call them 'doctors'.

'The most fundamental principle of medicine is Love.'

—Paracelsus (1493–1541)

Prologue

Chronicles of a Gynaecologist had been out for more than a year now and I was basking in the success of becoming a doctor-author. My first book focussed on two sections of society I fought passionately for, women and doctors. The book was about the gynaecologist and her patient. But, what made a doctor, and particularly a gynaecologist?

'You want to become a doctor?' I remembered my relatives looking shocked! A thin, small-built girl, who easily got scared by just about everything, no one believed I had it in me to become a doctor.

'I wouldn't be touching lizards and cockroaches.' I would defend.

'You will need to do surgery, deal with blood.' Their eyes widened as they recalled my histrionics during vaccinations.

My immature mind got influenced by the doctors I came across. Their world seemed so glamorous. I gave up on my dreams to become an engineer and my father gave up on his of seeing me as a bureaucrat, at least temporarily.

But then the next few years took me on a fascinating, whirlwind of a journey. And, every other ambition of mine got trampled on this rollercoaster ride.

I wanted the world to know the metamorphosis and soon started writing my next manuscript, *Anecdotes of a Medico*. I wanted to share all that went behind making a doctor. From working with cadavers to real patients, from overbearing seniors to those who shaped your career, I wanted to deliver the truths that breathed behind the closed, sanitised walls of a hospital, exposing the sad realities that plague our society. These were troubled times, where so much was being said everywhere that 'truth' became a myth. The book would give a broad perspective of the factors that interplay in the making of a doctor.

Above all, I wanted this book to be a bridge between the medical and the non-medical world.

And, then one day I was invited by my alma mater, the Gajra Raja Medical College, Gwalior, to give of talk on my first book. I was overjoyed. It was a feeling of déjà vu, to take my book to where it all started, sharing with those who had been my co-passengers in this enlightening journey.

I met my head of department, my teachers and my seniors. The department of obstetrics and gynaecology! It was nostalgic. I was standing at that phase of life where I had left them years ago. I understood them more! My juniors had flourished over the years. So many memories came gushing. So many untold stories came rushing into my mind.

And, the old hospital building...it stared at me!

I was transported back. This place had single-handedly taken me away from everything safe and secure, everything I once believed in and sucked me like a tornado into a new world. A world infested with pain, suffering and disease; blood, gore and disbelief, a world inhabited by patients and doctors, nurses and staff. A world that made you its backbone, a world that clung on your shaky shoulders.

A world that challenged you as you struggled with stereotypes and misogyny. It frustrated as much with prejudices and the social bigotry as the fury wrecked by anaemia, haemorrhage, eclampsia and unsafe abortions. The pain of seeing young lives lost to preventable diseases left deep scars. The septic labour room and the eclampsia room still formed my worst nightmares! No wonder they keep cropping up prominently in my narratives.

Now, years later, after having moved to Delhi, whenever I see the same diseases surrendering in front of advancements in medicine and technology, better blood products and better intensive care, I get gripped with regret and an intense sense of loss.

And, I missed my emergency duties. The times when we were the unquestionable boss. There was something so comforting about seeing the hospitals at night, swathed in yellow light, minus the hustle bustle of the day. With relatives gone home and most patients sleeping; the emergency staff beating their biological clock and still looking energetic, the building looked almost inviting. At times the peace and serenity belied the tensions underneath as if the hospital wanted to forget its turbulent activities and sleep over its daylong turmoil. And, as one welcomed 'life' in the early hours after the night had 'laboured' long enough, nothing could beat the morning cup of tea!

The aroma of fresh tea intermingled with the flavour of duty of the past 24 hours, as we residents from different departments sneaked out to the tea stall just opposite the hospital gate, lingered in my memories.

With every nerve of the body crying 'go to sleep', barely after a two-hour break, we dragged our sleep-deprived yet widely awake minds to our assigned wards. Yet, nothing could measure up to the sense of accomplishment that an emergency duty imbibed.

The frequent tiffs with the administration still bring an indulgent smile on my face. Our blood boiled at the slightest provocation yet cooled down with just an affectionate pat. Always in the line of fire from seniors, teachers, administrators and patients, yet we laughed freely and fought back fiercely.

'*Aap duty pe sone ke liye aate hai* (Do you come to sleep at work)?' An elderly man in a cream kurta-pajama had once sneered down at our fellow resident.

Tired after being on toes for more than 16 hours, he had decided to stretch his neck muscles at around 2 am. He had hardly rested his head on the desk when a bright light dazzled his tired eyes.

He flushed guiltily. Just his luck that a new, overzealous minister was on his nocturnal, surprise tour of the hospital. What better way to gain public mileage than by snooping on a doctor! It made great news for the next few weeks. The poor doctor was suspended. The residents who were the backbone of the hospitals were ridiculed and made scapegoats by the spineless politicians and an insensitive media. What followed was a strike down by the RDA (Resident Doctors' Association) till the suspension was cancelled and the doctor reinstated.

The medicos were notorious for getting into a broil with just about anyone, the bureaucrats, the police or even the goons. We feared none! This was, after all, the land of the Chambal.

And it gave back so much more. It gave me the passion to stick to my conviction, the compassion to deal with disease and infirmities, the zeal to fight the Almighty, the steel to take on my destiny, the mettle to override my fears and insecurities, the nerve to hold back my tears and bid goodbye.

This place also gave me love, my life and friends for a lifetime.

Post-graduation was a time of building relationships.

I watched the corridors with awe. I had matched steps with Sameer, sneaked into his ward, held his hands and looked into his eyes with a promise. Dousing hopes of my parents to find a bureaucrat match for their daughter, I was rewriting my destiny on a blank sheet.

And I had laughed here with my friends—Kavya, Raj, Varun, Ranjan, Meera and Parul amongst many others! The silly banter, the juicy gossip, rushing off from the hospital to watch the first day-first show at the movies, sitting in the first row! I had evolved with them, cried out my disappointments over their shoulders, clasped their hand to tide over many a crisis. We had worked together as if driven, pitched against odds that tested every fibre of our body and had emerged victorious.

Between ignorant, innocent patients to the vindictive ones, between crumbling health infrastructure, dwindling resources to the tenacious, budding doctors, between bullying seniors to those who held your hands and taught, between friends and family who got sidelined to the ones who stood by you even in your worst 'complications'; between the samosa and tea breaks to the forgotten lunches, between sleep-deprived nights to an all-time high of saving lives, between forgotten marriages to love blossoming in the wards...there was something that broke through. The first cry of 'life' as it opened its beautiful eyes!

And as we took our baby steps, the 'hospital' watched patiently and heralded the birth of a new being. A gynaecologist!

These were my most cherished memories, my most prized possession.

So, *Anecdotes of a Medico* took a backseat. This story had to be told first. My brush with this institution, the Kamla Raja Hospital and the department of obstetrics and gynaecology!

I entered again, the 'house of doctors'.

Introduction

My earliest memory of the department of obstetrics and gynaecology is not a particular patient or a particular doctor but a strong smell and a mad commotion. The smell still stays and sometimes when I visit a government hospital, it takes me on a memory trail. I cannot pinpoint for sure what the smell was about. May be the red, overused Mackintosh that lay on the beds or the sweaty sheets and clothes in which the patient travelled miles before reaching the hospitals. It could also be about the amniotic fluid swarming the labour room or even the stinking bathrooms. It remained buried deep in my mind. Our senses adapted to it, to the extent that we looked with disdain at others trying to cover their nose in the hospital.

And the commotion! Be it at the gate of the Kamla Raja Hospital, the entry to the labour room, outside the operation theatre or within the wards. The expressions were almost universal—anxiety, apprehension, restlessness giving rise to sometimes relief and sadly sometimes to grief and a sense of loss.

The department was unique. Here, majority of the patients were suffering not from a pathology, but an altered physiology. Those pacing outside the labour wards and operation theatres were the ones waiting for some 'good news'. Yet, there were dangers lurking round the corner. Obstetrics remained an unpredictable branch. It didn't take much for things to change dramatically catching even the doctor unawares. However, it was a dynamic department, the only fast-paced place in a hospital. And the only place where people celebrated, the arrival of life! People distributed sweets here and carried memories of having first held in their arms, a gift from God, a token of their love.

Hospitals were also a striking proof of the fast growing population of this country. They were also proof of our aptitude to gossip endlessly. In India, talking is the strongest antidote to most sufferings, much stronger than any medicine. You could easily spot them neck-deep into it, sharing their grievances which could range from their mothers-in-law, their medical problems to their misgivings about the care being given, the doctors, the hospitals and yes, the food.

It was hilarious that even a couple of days in the hospital equipped them with enough knowledge to give a medical advice. One pregnancy made you an obstetrician, one baby a paediatrician and one visit to the hospital an 'all-round' physician for a lifetime. The free advices, especially the medical ones, although unasked for, were usually looked at with more respect and trust than even a paid medical advice. These were also the places where doctors were graded, the best ones decided, swapped and the referrals done.

People travelled from places not just with their patients but also with their stoves and grocery, despite repeated warnings by the security staff. The aroma of fresh food being cooked in the hospital corridors whetted everyone's appetites. The bias that people carried about hospital food was clearly evident in the leftovers ravaged by the dogs and cats that were the permanent residents of the hospitals.

There was one thing the cats loved more than food. But I will come to that later for I don't want to offend the senses of my readers in the beginning. Moreover, it was much later that I discovered it.

The beautiful doctors were, however, the brightest aspect of this department. The elegant doctors were known not just for style, fashion and glamour but also for 'substance'. The zeal with which they rushed about invoked respect. I envied their energy.

You could easily spot in the department a harassed-looking girl, sprinting past, with her hair flying everywhere, patience snapping from the lack of sleep the night before yet trying to keep up with the pace of the day. She would be seen trying to match the steps of the doctor on rounds, clutching a bundle of papers as they fell around, jotting down the flurry of advice from her senior to sometimes silently looking around for that 'forever' and miraculously disappearing pen. And once the rounds were over you could also catch her giggling over a cup of tea and a hot samosa with her friends. These were the brief interludes in the life of a resident doctor.

There was another 'trademark' of a gynae resident—a tote, almost the size of a travelling bag, which they fancifully called a kit. It contained all the stuff you would need for an emergency surgery or an emergency delivery. From stationary like blank papers, requisition forms to intravenous sets, Foley's catheters and sutures, it had everything. A smart resident came with a smart, well-equipped kit. Not everything was available in the hospital and neither every patient who walked in could afford all the items. A lot of times, this kit was the sole saving grace in acute emergencies and life-threatening situations.

The kit also taught the finer nuances of management. When a patient of normal delivery was asked to buy a Foley's catheter that she would not need instead of the more expensive suture given free you knew it was the 'kit' calling. Most of the attendants were not literate enough to understand this 'barter' in its most enterprising form. It was a patient paying for another patient. The chances of your senior bashing for that absent Foley's catheter in your kit was more worrisome than an attendant complaining. The idea was to keep the kit surplus and to replace what was disappearing, irrespective of the cost. That was the need of the hour and the insight of the resident. Needless to say, the kit was the most precious commodity in the hospital. Patients owed more to the smart kit and a resourceful resident than to the hospital and the government.

Those were blessed times. The media stayed where it belonged, in the newsrooms. People thronged the hospitals with trust. And for the doctors, the concerns of their patients were paramount.

Our first exposure to the gynaecology wards was during the third-year clinical postings in the department. Conventionally, the second-year post-graduates took our classes during the afternoon posting. Post-graduation in the obstetrics and gynaecology department was of three years. The first-year PG was called a House Surgeon, second-year the Junior RSO (Resident Surgical Officer) and the third-year PG was called the Senior RSO.

There was much more to learn from these wards and the hospital in general for the discerning eye but most of the times the students were busy in themselves, gossiping just as much as the attendants whom they pushed as they made their way past, unmindful of their glares.

In my final year, where it was a main subject, I would return to the department again for a longer time. I would need to grasp it better for I would need to clear the subject in my final professional exams. Later in my internship, I would come here again, hopefully to have some hands on experience but most of the times for the much pricey attendance.

My post-graduation would take me on an undefined journey, where there would be no rules but new boundaries. My rendezvous with this branch would threaten to redefine my life. No wonder it is the longest and the deepest section of this book. I will have to delve deep because only then will I come up with this gem, my most treasured belonging—MS (Obstetrics & Gynaecology); my identity henceforth.

But all this would come later.

For now it was the 'hospital' calling the third years.

Third Year

'Every physician must be rich in knowledge, and not only of that which is written in books; his patients should be his book, they will never mislead him.'

—Paracelsus

'Sister, where would the labour ward be?' He stopped in front of us and asked, a little unsure. The harassed-looking man was trying to locate his patient.

Kavya looked offended while the boys laughed. Our white aprons made us stand out, but clearly not enough!

'I am not sister!' She replied pointedly and walked away. This was one line that would be repeated over and over again and we had yet to perfect the act of ignoring it.

The poor guy had no clue about the offence he had committed.

'*Bhaiyya,* let me explain this to you.' Taking pity on him Raj started giving him with the directions.

Before he could complete a loud scream broke through the corridor. The visitor didn't need the directions anymore. It was coming right from the labour room itself. We rushed towards the source of the noise.

The entry was clogged. We peered through the crowd. Our white coats helped us make our way through.

'Stay away from me.' A woman was standing on the labour table. Her intravenous (IV) set dangled from her hand and the IV stand was about to fall when the ward *bai* lunged forward. By then the IV line had been disconnected.

'Oh my god!' The doctor stared at the blood that started oozing from the intravenous set. The labour-room nurse leapt to hold her wrist, another two people, probably her relatives, grabbed her before the venflon could be closed to stop the gushing blood.

'Let me go!' Unmindful of everyone the woman shrieked.

The poor doctor was out of her wits.

I had been warned by almost everyone right from my seniors to friends and family about the labour room. Seriously, I didn't know that it would be so dramatic.

But what exactly was going on here?

'She had a normal delivery. There is a vaginal tear that needs to be stitched but she wants to go home, unstitched,' the labour-room doctor informed us. We looked at her surprised.

'Can't we do it under anaesthesia? Why strain her if she is so reluctant?' I asked.

'She needs to come down, even for that.' The nurse chipped in.

'Listen, your stitches will get infected and will never heal.' The doctor tried to reason out with her.

'*Aadmi paas nahi ayega* (Your man will not come near you).' The ward *bai* added.

We looked at each other. This was crude.

'I don't care.' She shouted.

Meanwhile, her husband and mother-in-law were called in. From cajoling to threatening they tried out everything but in vain. She refused to budge.

'It's all because of you!' She started abusing them and fed up, they went out.

Her hair flew around her face wildly and her clothes were still scattered around her body but she was unabashed and looked possessed.

'I think she's hysterical.' Raj whispered.

'Maybe she's burnt out by the pain.' The doctor was still sympathetic.

The woman, meanwhile, stared mutinously even as she chose to finally sit down on the labour table.

'Husband *se milti ho to dard nahi hota* (Doesn't it pain when you have sex with your husband)?' We gasped at another profanity from the ward *bai*.

Was this what everyone warned us about?

'You shall learn the basics from the labour room.' Our seniors had told us.

'You are not even allowed to be embarrassed. There are male doctors there, too. But you can't protest.' I remembered my mother telling me her scary story. Was it really 'a house of horror'?

And the patient clearly had had enough. She wanted to go home.

'You will have to sign this before you go.'

She readily signed on the paper that she was refusing all treatment and was going home on her own wish. This was called LAMA, left against medical advice.

A little bemused, we started ascending the stairs towards the lecture theatre. The aroma of freshly brewed coffee from the office of the head of the department welcomed us as we made our way to the lecture hall. The official rooms of the consultants lay adjacent to the lecture hall.

By now we were adept at picking up the fragrance coming from the rooms and identifying the consultant.

Dr Sarika entered the classroom.

'Good afternoon.' She greeted cheerfully. Taking out a chalk from the pocket of her apron she wrote: Obstetrics & Gynaecology.

'Not again.' The girls groaned.

This was the third class where the definitions were going to be taught. Dr Sarika pretended to have not heard our reaction. She turned around and pointed to one of the boys.

'Define obstetrics.'

He stared at her while rest of the boys laughed.

'Alright, gynaecology?' Dr Sarika asked, seeing his blank face.

He fumbled and looked around for support. The exasperated teacher asked the next boy.

'You?'

He looked back so stupidly that everyone burst out laughing.

'Keep quiet, everyone.' Dr Sarika was clearly getting impatient.

She then pointed to Kavya sitting on the front bench.

'Ma'am, obstetrics is the branch of medicine that deals with pregnancy and childbirth.' She answered confidently.

'Gynaecology?'

'It is the branch of medicine that deals with the problems of the female genital tract.'

'That was pretty simple, wasn't it? Why don't you boys listen?' Dr Sarika said.

They were still not listening.

'Ma'am, we are not going to take up this branch.' They grinned shamelessly.

The gender bias was obvious. Out of the many subjects taught as undergraduates one would pursue only one as a postgraduate. Yet, the way boys treated gynaecology was so uniformly similar that it became pathetic.

'Aren't you supposed to clear the subject in your undergraduate exams?' Dr Sarika asked.

The boys looked away.

It was an undisputed fact that the boys were treated leniently in the department. Most of them were here for the sake of attendance and to have some fun. Even then it was clear where their priorities lay, definitely not in the subject but always in the petite doctors.

They had been very well tuned by their seniors on how to behave here. If any boy showed interest in the subject, he was immediately labelled 'sissy' and was much ridiculed later in the hostel.

Not every girl dreamt of becoming a gynaecologist and there were quite a handful who believed that their interests lay beyond the functioning of the female genital tract. It was definitely not their cup of tea. But there was another universal truth. A woman could take up any speciality but to the public she would always be a 'lady doctor' and that meant an obstetrician by default.

Invariably, most female doctors, whatever branch they opted for, were forced to practice gynaecology especially in the smaller cities. It became easier for them to establish their practice. But, times were changing. Obstetrics was tough, demanding and a very challenging branch fraught with litigations. There was money but it came at a cost. Most gynaecologists paid it with their time. No wonder many young doctors were now opting for safer pastures which gave them a better quality of life.

Besides, medical colleges reeked of gender discrimination. Girls couldn't dream of entering the male domain of general surgery, medicine, orthopaedics amongst many others. Most of the branches barring obstetrics and gynaecology were male-centric. Acceptance by the general public was also very poor. A male surgeon always carried more weight than a female one. People didn't trust females in any branch besides obstetrics and gynaecology, more so as surgeons.

A female doctor was called 'sister' but a male doctor was always doctor sahib. Even his wife was *doctorni*.

Dr Sarika, meanwhile, had moved on to the next question.

'What is gravida and what is para?' She looked around questioning.

Again, this was the third class that we were discussing it. Would we ever move to anything else?

'Ma'am, can't we go and see some patients? We have already been through this so many times.' One of the girls asked.

'Then answer my question fast and we will,' Dr Sarika said.

'Gravida (G) refers to the number of conceptions and para (P) to the number of deliveries. So a first-time pregnant woman would be G1P0.' The girls were in no mood to let the boys stall the class again.

'So, a pregnant woman with one previous abortion and no live issue is G2P0A1.' Dr Sarika went on elaborating.

'It looks more like some coded message.' Sameer rued.

Clinical history taking was much different in gynaecology. Here, one had to go in details into obstetric and menstrual history.

The issue of gravida and para was closed for the time being. It would come to haunt us again in our final year in medical college. But, right now we wanted to see a 'real' patient. We had enough of theory classes.

Looking at the excited faces, Dr Sarika took us to the antenatal wards. They generally kept the patients with complicated pregnancy here. The 'patient' came to sit before the students reluctantly. It was one thing being doctor in the eyes of the neighbours and relatives but it was something else commanding respect in the eyes of these patients. They knew better, the worth of young medicos. Predictably, this one carried a bored expression.

'I was going to rest.' She lamented.

'I hope you had your lunch.' Dr Sarika spoke indulgently.

'The food was not even good today.' She continued to crib. 'My mother is going to come today with some home-cooked food. My son will come along too. Please allow them to meet me.' The deal was sealed. She knew the ball was in her court. The art of 'bartering' was not lost to the patients either.

She was an experienced patient, one who knew her answers well. She informed us that she was about 36 weeks pregnant. Calculating the gestation in months was taboo. Conventionally, the expected due date (EDD) was derived by adding nine months and seven days to the last menstrual period (LMP). Sounds simple, doesn't it?

'The examiner will flunk you if you calculate her period of gestation in months.' Dr Sarika warned.

'Why make everything so complicated? What difference would that make, anyway?' whispered an aggrieved voice.

'So how many weeks would be if she has completed nine months?' Dr Sarika was looking pointedly at Sameer.

'Thirty-six weeks.' Sameer was quick to reply.

'Really? Every month has only four weeks?'

'Of course!'

Dr Sarika raised an eyebrow.

Sameer flushed.

'Err.'

'It is four weeks and three or two days.' Sameer lowered his eyes.

'So, now you know. On your due date you complete almost 40 weeks.'

A lesson one was never likely to forget.

Dr Sarika went on to demonstrate the four obstetric grips to explain to us the position and presentation of the baby which was now called foetus. The top fundal grip to feel the head, lateral (side) grips to feel the back, the pelvic (lower) grips to feel the head which was the presenting part (the part that comes out first) in the majority of cases.

As she made us do those grips, we almost felt like a real doctor, the difference being that we hardly understood much but well, the patient wouldn't know that. Or would she?

One could just marvel at the difference this touch of a patient brought to the budding doctors. While most of us were trying our best to absorb this clinical acumen and waited excitedly for our turn, Raj looked a little hesitant. It started with the first grip but as he reached the lower pelvic grip, his discomfort became almost visible.

'What's wrong with you?' Kavya looked at him with curiosity.

'How can you girls be so insensitive?' He looked concerned.

'I could almost feel that I had gripped the baby's neck in the pelvic grip. What if we really strangulated it? I have such strong hands.' He was deeply worried. This had never crossed anybody's mind.

Dr Sarika burst out laughing.

'Don't worry. Maybe now I need to prove that you have not harmed the baby.'

She brought the stethoscope on the patient's abdomen and made us listen. A sound which was almost like a horse galloping filled the room. So fast and so rhythmic! Everyone took turns and listened, completely enthralled. A sense of peace and contentment enveloped all faces. It was strange; this effect a foetal heartbeat could have on, not just the mother but everyone, even the errant boys. It was almost as if it was reassuring that the human species was growing, safe and protected.

'The baby can communicate with the external world through this single sound. It can convey that it is distressed and needs to be taken out fast,' Dr Sarika said.

'And also the havoc it creates in the lives of not just the patient but the doctor too when it goes missing.' She warned.

Third-year clinics were only about basics. It was more about getting familiar with the subject. History taking, routine obstetric examination, mechanism of normal labour and some important medical conditions complicating pregnancy like anaemia and high blood pressure. But yes, one just couldn't escape abortion and contraception. It was taught in almost every year of medicine in some way or other. This was probably to reinforce the young minds with what they would soon realise was the 'felt need' of India.

The clinic was a place where one could really comprehend what ailed one half of the population.

Most women were obsessed with one organ of their body—the mysterious womb or the uterus! From something as vague as a simple backache, to something as weird as mood changes, everything they suffered was somehow related to it. And then there were milestones.

'My backache started after my son was born.' The problems could be traced back to their pregnancy period.

And the most common grievance was undisputedly the shortcomings of their 'in laws' and husband during that period. 'Never got to rest and nobody took care of me.' Not that they were always wrong.

But most women had been there and done that. The easy familiarity with the condition often made them casual to other women. It often masked an attitude to neglect.

However, it was also here that one met the most sacrificing, most loving specie that God ever made, women!

My friend Kavya and I made our way with difficulty through the noisy corridors lined with women waiting for their turn. It was always very difficult to control women deep in gossip, engrossed as they were in more pertinent issues. Like the saree they bought, the recipe they had tried, the hundred ways to make a simple *dal*, the *saas-bahu* soap operas, the men in their lives to the common ogre in all women's lives, their mothers-in-law. The older ones generally looked with disdain at the young doctors. '*Inko kya samajh mein ayega* (What will they understand)!'

In crisp, white aprons with a stethoscope hanging proudly around our neck, we settled down in the outdoor clinic. Our senior, a house surgeon briefed us. Armed with our theoretical knowledge we set on our maiden mission.

'Prabhadevi, how old are you?' Age was very important in the medical history.

It was seemingly a simple question, but then was it really easy?

'Must be 30–32 years.' She definitely looked much more than that.

The house surgeon interrupted.

'How many children?'

'Four, Sir.'

'Sir' was often gender neutral in hospitals. It was better than being called sister.

'How old is the eldest?'

'Twenty-five years.'

There, she couldn't be five years old when she had her first baby! Some fast calculations, the age of her marriage and the ages of all her children it was reasonably deduced that she had to be at least 45. To the lady it hardly mattered. Age was probably just a number.

'So what are your complains?' The doctor asked.

She looked around, covering her head with her saree's *pallu* a little more securely. She was looking for some support. Her husband stood at the door. It was better to ignore him, rather prudent to elicit history from the patient herself. That would be the real test to what we were learning, the art of taking medical history!

'If you can't tell us we will send you out again.' The house surgeon spoke a little firmly.

She looked outside, hesitated and began reluctantly.

'*Aadmi se baat karne mein taklif hoti hai* (It pains to talk to my man).'

Now, what kind of problem was this? Were we supposed to solve their domestic problems as well?

'Listen, medical problem *batao*.'

'Madam, *bas yahi hai*.' She covered her face some more and fixed her gaze on the floor.

'*Arrey*, then stop talking to him *na*.' That was easy enough.

'Madam, *woh manta nahi hai. Bolta hai bahar chala jaunga* (He doesn't listen. Says he will move out).'

This was getting weird. Suddenly someone nudged and the outdoor slip was pulled away by the house surgeon.

'*Kabse hai* (Since when)?' She asked.

'For more than a year.' She replied without lifting her gaze.

'Painful coitus for one year.' The senior deftly wrote on the outdoor slip.

Talking implied so much more. A 'lingo' that was going to be a useful aid in the future.

We focussed back to the patient who was still being questioned.

'Last period date?' She kept looking at the doctor and then looked across at her husband.

It was more sensible to call him now, limited that our knowledge was with the Hindi months. Moreover LMP—not known, usually signified the doctor's incapability at history taking more than the patient's answering capability.

Her husband walked in folding his hands.

'March 22, Madam.' He had been listening.

As he went in detailing about her obstetrical and menstrual history we marvelled at the depth of his knowledge and awareness.

'Why couldn't she tell all this?'

'Madam, *padhi likhi nahi hai na* (She is not educated).'

The wives could be entrusted with their kids but not with their own medical history. It was so difficult to understand how the dynamics worked but then that was how majority Indian families functioned.

She was taken inside for check-up and soon her prescription was ready.

The medicines were explained to her in detail. But it was evident that things had to be repeated to the husband for reasons more than one.

The senior clarified. 'Most women take pride in not understanding anything. They will listen to your advice very seriously before requesting you to repeat all of it to their husband or their mother-in-law. Probably to them, they are the more intelligent people but I think it is just a smart move on their part for putting all accountability on someone else.'

'*Apas mein ek mahine tak baat nahi karna* (Don't'talk to each other for a month).' That was a doctor's advice for abstinence. The patient nodded.

'Abstinence has to be reinforced to her husband, especially after surgery. If they report to the hospital bleeding it's you who shall never be forgiven for that.' The house surgeon warned.

The next patient was a little more enterprising.

'Do you have any complains?'

'No, Madam.'

You never went to a hospital without complains. We probed further.

'Backache, lack of appetite, nausea.' No gynaecological complains. Should she be referred to a physician?

Once again the house surgeon came to our rescue.

'When did you have your last period?' The house surgeon asked.

'Madam, two months back.'

How could a doctor look at their faces and know that they were pregnant. That was expecting too much.

It was not easy when you were pitched up against the high standards set by the filmy doctors who held the pulse of a fainting heroine and announced the good news. The celluloid doctor with his briefcase and gut instincts, and the benchmarks they set for the 'real' doctors were hard to match!

What rescued the doctors more often was common sense even though it remained a precious commodity. It taught so much more, beyond medical textbooks.

A good doctor was supposed to be well versed in the local dialect. Nothing came handier for a gynaecologist than a thorough knowledge of the name of all the months in Hindi.

Interestingly, *Sawan* and *Bhado* were the easiest months to know in Hindi, thanks to the rain sequence in the song, '*Mere naina sawan bhado...*'. It had to be the monsoon months of July and August. But it was not just the names of months, a smart resident was supposed to remember all the festivals dates, even months after they had actually happened.

The easy ones told you that they had periods during Holi, the mind teasers were the ones who said, '*Mahina charte Chait mein aaya tha* (Had menses in the beginning of the Hindi month of Chait)!'

If you think your degree and your white coat placed you at a higher pedestal, some patients were going to teach you otherwise.

'Is this your first pregnancy?'

She kept quiet.

'Rani, kitne bachche hain (Rani, how many kids do you have)?' Every day the third years were getting smarter. Calling the patients *'Rani'* was one such move.

Arrogance was a virtue that seeped in quietly especially when you were the ones running the show and the medicos were no exception.

'Two.'

'So this is your third pregnancy.'

'Nahi, Madam*ji,* fifth.'

Damn the confusion! Where was I going wrong here?

'When you ask about *"bachche"* they will always tell you about their sons. The daughters are never mentioned. You have to be very specific when you ask about daughters. Let me show you.' Again our senior intervened.

'Rani, kitne ladke aur kitni ladkiyan (How many boys and how many girls)?'

'Two boys and two girls.'

So many children! She actually didn't look very well to do either.

'They have a lot of money. It's we who have to struggle for every single penny.' The house surgeon added sarcastically.

'Mera pati kamata hai. Humko khilayega, tumko kya (My husband earns. He will feed us. Why do you worry)?' She pushed her *pallu* back and snapped.

Not all patients fed your ego. Some matched your arrogance too.

The patient scowled and turned away sulking. 'This time I will get the ligation done.' Ligation was the sterilisation operation.

'And, of course get the money and enjoy other incentives!' The house surgeon exclaimed.

'Why now, after four children when she has already destroyed the country's resources?' She muttered, low enough so that the patient did not hear. But the third years could and reeled at the unfairness. Fortunately, it was tea time.

'Where is the intern?' The house surgeon looked around.

The intern had an interesting duty that was not negotiable. They were the ones who brought samosas, a tradition that few departments were willing to break. This was the time to be relished as we closed the door to the complaining relatives for a ten-minute reprieve. Everything was forgotten as we got down to famishing the delicious, hot samosas.

Though the juniors never paid, they were often made to treat the seniors. First experiences were always celebrated. First deliveries, first suturing, first surgery or any procedure, even as vague as first pelvic examination to the first Copper-T insertion or removal, the seniors never missed out the 'samosa' opportunity. Though the junior residents were the usual preys, sometimes an over enthusiastic, unsuspecting medico fell into the trap. It was a bad omen to refuse and most of the juniors looked forward to this ritual.

The tea break had barely finished when the door was thrust open and a villager pushed his wife inside.

'We have been waiting since early morning.' He looked disapprovingly at the vestiges of our samosa party.

'Have patience, everybody's turn will come. Doctors also need to eat.' Our OPD attendant scolded him.

The patient came to sit quietly on a stool near the house surgeon.

'I can't conceive. We have been going in circles for ages.' She looked distressed.

The doctor looked at her previous reports and then sent her inside for a check-up. Her husband waited outside, still looking impatient.

'What the hell is this?' A startled voice came from inside.

'This' was her vagina smeared outrageously with an orangish-red colour powder. Traces of ash could also be seen there. The bewildered doctor stood next to her.

The patient kept quiet and turned her head away, clearly evasive.

The husband was called inside.

'What is going on?' The doctor asked.

'It's a simple ritual. Early in the morning, I have to smear her vagina with vermillion and then chant a few mantras holding an *agarbatti* (incense stick) near it.' Her husband declared.

'What!'

'Madam, we were fed up of going to doctors. With no result coming out of it all, a family friend suggested us this *tantrik.*' He looked at us defensively.

At any other time we could have all laughed at this. But, right now all we felt was a deep aversion.

'It doesn't harm us nor does it cost much. Maybe this will help where all medicines fail.' The husband added.

'*Dekho bhaiyya*, you can say your prayers but please don't burn her. That will add to your problems.' The doctor said.

It was difficult to shake off deep-seated faith people had on alternative medicines and religious gurus. It would only bring out antagonism.

The house surgeon wrote down a battery of tests for the patient. She quietly left with her husband.

'Our biggest rivals are these *babas* and alternative medicine. If by mere coincidence, this woman becomes pregnant, this *baba*'s status shall ascend next to God! And, he would amass wealth too!' The house surgeon sighed.

'We are going to be taught the mechanism of labour on a dummy.' Kavya informed us. The dummy was called '*gudda*-pelvis'.

The baby till it was inside the mother was technically a 'foetus'. And '*gudda*' was the name given to the stuffed doll that would be used as a foetus. It was stitched by the first-year postgraduates every successive year, cared for and fussed over like a baby by the students and residents alike. Pelvis, the birth canal, was something we were familiar with after having studied it in much detail in anatomy in the first professional.

Here, the *gudda*-pelvis was a couple and was treated with reverence.

'Today, we shall comprehend the dynamics of their togetherness.' Our teacher said. 'You need to be familiar with the path very thoroughly. Imagine, how difficult it was for the foetus to negotiate its way through the birth canal,' she added.

Life was never easy. The foetus realised it as soon as it started its maiden journey to move out of its first shelter to the real world outside. With lots of twists on the way, the journey was long and fraught with dangers and adventures before the baby could let out its first cry and be held in the warm, secure embrace of its mother.

'The baby lies curled up, all joints in complete flexion. During descent, the head rotates internally as it reaches the pelvic floor just below the pubic arch. You can now see the head.' The teacher explained.

It sounded so exciting.

'Soon there is extension of the head as it comes out, rotating externally as the shoulders come in the line followed by the lateral (side) flexion to deliver the whole body.'

We listened with awe. At any step things could go terribly wrong. And, on board this divine journey, the foetus was as time bound as everything else in this material world.

Labour was conventionally divided in three stages. The management for every stage was different. Neither the foetus nor the mother could linger at one stage forever. There were deadlines!

'The sun should not rise and set twice on a woman in labour.' This was a dictum that had been followed through generations.

We were yet to grasp the gravity of this African dictum but would soon realise that in a far-flung, diverse country like ours women first laboured at home or sometimes in a primary health centre before they gave up and got referred. They then travelled miles to reach the referral hospital. Prolonged and obstructed labour had damaging consequences even for those who made it. Some were scarred forever and some leaked forever from the non-healing fistulas between the vagina and the bladder, a sure shot sign of the paucity of resources and a crumbling healthcare and delivery system especially in rural India.

As third-year medical students we were not expected to know much about abnormal labour. It was more than enough to know the normal things at this stage of learning.

'Every labour is a trial of labour. Some ended up as caesarean. And not all foetuses made it successfully. Sadly, neither did all mothers.' Our teacher said.

Women continued to die around the world because of pregnancy-related complications. India had a very high maternal mortality rate. Anaemia, high blood pressure, haemorrhages and unsafe abortions were the leading causes. The learning years at Kamla Raja Hospital, Gwalior, left us in no doubts and told exactly why and how they killed pregnant women.

Third year had limited postings in the gynaecology department and for the next few days we were posted in the labour room. This was the most dynamic, the most happening place in the hospital.

At the entry a women lay on a stretcher. She wore a dirty saree and a strange smell enveloped her.

'All of you move out.' The nurse shouted at the relatives. 'Please stay away.'

Another hugely pregnant woman was standing inside with her mother-in-law.

'The baby is not moving inside at all.' The mother-in-law complained.

'Did she eat something and rest?' Dr Seema, the resident on duty asked the patient.

'*Arrey,* we tried everything.'

'Did you give her something sweet to eat?'

'Glucose instantly kicks the babies.' Dr Seema explained to us.

'All our family members have been shaking her whole body. What will food do when that hasn't worked?'

They all had taken turns in shaking her just to make the baby move! Strange logic!

'Who has asked you to do that? You all could have caused more harm than good.' Dr Seema looked angry.

'Our *behenji* told us to do that.' There were people besides doctors advising them. *Behenji* was their village *dai.*

Dr Seema made the patient lie down on the table. Fortunately, the foetal heartbeat was present. She sighed with relief and sent her for an ultrasound.

'We need to be sure that the placenta has not separated in all the jerky movements.' She explained, shaking her head in disgust at them.

'But she does have a point, if you move the mother as per the law of physics, everything inside her should move.' Raj wondered.

'So as per the law of physics I should shake you up to move your brain up there.' Varun countered back, pointing towards Raj's head.

Meanwhile, the relatives of the patient lying outside on the stretcher tried to push inside the already packed labour room. All of them claimed to be her close relatives and wanted to stay with her. Finally, the security guard was called in and the crowd cleared. The woman was brought inside. As she lay down on the examination bed, she groaned.

'One of you check her vitals.' The resident on duty, Dr Seema said while she took a quick history.

'She is nine months pregnant and has travelled from Dholpur.'

'Ma'am is she having labour pains?' We were curious.

'Yes, you can feel the abdomen tighten along with the pain. It's the uterine contraction.' She made us palpate as we touched her in wonder.

'It comes and goes, increasing in frequency and intensity.'

'The problem is that along with all this the patient has severe anaemia.' She looked at her with mild trepidation.

This happened to be her third pregnancy; the previous two were all home deliveries.

'Do you women even think that if something goes wrong with you who will look after your children?' Dr Seema sounded exasperated.

The patient smiled weakly and looked away.

'You can only pity her.' Dr Seema shook her head. 'We live in a country where women hardly have any reproductive rights.'

Her haemoglobin was 5 gm. Even to those who lacked the clinical acumen to judge her haemoglobin concentration clinically, it was apparent. She looked deathly pale.

'Bring your own palms and compare with hers.' Dr Seema placed her own palm next to that of the patient. Even at a haemoglobin of 10 gm, her palm was shinning pink in front of the shocking white of the patient.

'Our own hands can serve as the quickest way of assessing anaemia.' We grasped that quickly.

'But she was gaining weight.' Her relatives appeared surprised.

'The patient was oedematous, all swollen up as happens in severe anaemia due to water retention.' Dr Seema explained to them.

'I had no problem, so I never visited a doctor.' The patient admitted hesitantly.

Were women indeed better than livestock? There were no antenatal checkups till one day she landed up at the district hospital complaining of breathlessness.

'The district hospital lacked a blood bank and facilities to handle a high-risk pregnancy. So they immediately referred me to a higher centre for further management.' Short of breath, she spoke with much difficulty.

'She is just 25 years old and this is her third pregnancy.' Dr Seema said.

'That made her G3P2,' we added.

Dr Seema smiled.

'The pulse rate is a little high, but her other vitals are stable. She needs urgent blood transfusion before labour strains her already compromised system,' Dr Seema said.

The blood bank in the medical college was reasonably stocked but then a government hospital suffers from an ever-widening gap between demand and supply. The deficit usually took its toll on not only the patients but the doctors as well.

Meanwhile, arrangements were being made for her urgent transfusion. Samples were withdrawn and sent.

'It is more important to explain to her relatives that she is critical. And then make them donate blood. That is usually our waterloo!' Dr Seema laughed.

She made a quick call to the blood bank in-charge.

'Ma'am, this time please arrange for this patient. She is A-positive. It's urgent.' Dr Seema was literally begging.

'Your cases always are.' The voice from the other side answered.

'I know we couldn't replace the last time but that one was bleeding. We just didn't have time.' Dr Seema continued to plead.

'I had spoken to her attendants and they promised to arrange blood. I know we owe you so much, Ma'am.'

'I understand, dear. But there have been no new donations in the last few days and we have exhausted all our stocks. We just have three units reserved for a patient who is going for surgery tomorrow. His relatives have already donated for him.' The blood-bank in-charge sounded worried.

She understood the pressures of the obstetrics department but then she had her own compulsions.

There were donors who wanted to earn money by selling blood, some out of poverty and some for buying drugs. She kept them out of the blood bank.

Relatives were seldom forthcoming for donations. Arranging camps and motivating people to replenish her meagre resources was the blood-bank incharge's saving grace. She had been successful to an extent, but one emergency like this took away all her stock in the fraction of a minute.

'Ma'am, this is an emergency. She is into labour and will die otherwise.' Dr Seema pleaded.

After much persuasion the blood-bank in-charge agreed. She had not much choice either. But she laid out the condition that the patient's family had to replace it by morning otherwise she would have to face the heat from the other patients' relatives.

Dr Seema quickly jotted down the high risk consent in Hindi. The security guard was sent to call her attendants again.

A thin, short woman wearing a dirty saree entered the room.

'Where is her husband?' Dr Seema asked.

'What happened? You can tell me.'

'Do you know she has very low haemoglobin? This means her life as well as that of the baby is in gross danger.'

The short woman folded her hands.

'We have come here only because of that. Her life is in your hands. I will send my son to sign the papers.'

As she started to walk outside, she was interrupted by Dr Seema.

'Listen, you have to arrange blood for her.'

'*Hum kahan se denge* (From where will we give)? We have no one to donate blood for her.'

'*Arrey*, a whole village has come with her. Call them now.'

'Which ones, Madam? I don't know them. They must be with other people. Please, *aap yahin se dila do* (You please arrange it from here only).'

'Do you want me to go and donate blood for every single patient? *Meri jaan le lo tum* (Just take my life).' Dr Seema had started getting irritated. There were other patients in the labour room too.

'If you can't arrange blood for her please take her away.' They had grown used to such relatives. There were at least five or six well-built, healthy attendants with her. But one call for blood, they all vanished into thin air.

'Madam, *hum mol le lenge* (We will pay the price).' She offered to buy blood.

'You please send her husband.' Dr Seema had had enough.

She reluctantly walked out.

Her husband was a healthy looking man, around 30.

'Sign here, please.' He quietly signed the high-risk form.

'You have two children at home. She is just 25 and her life is precious to them. We are trying to arrange blood for her, trying our level best to save her. Everything is free here. But even in a bank you have to deposit money before you take it out. Same way, even in a blood bank you have to deposit blood.'

He listened quietly, then looked at his wife anxiously.

'Can't we buy the blood, Madam?'

'That blood is just *Rooh Afza*. You cannot expect good haemoglobin from people who sell blood for money. This will not endanger your life. The blood you give gets replaced almost overnight.' Dr Seema reassured him.

'I am not a very strong person.' The robust-looking husband said.

'The blood bank will bleed you only if you are medically fit.'

'Okay, Madam, if you insist. I have no choice then.' He shrugged.

We didn't realise we had been holding our breath. This man had our earned respect.

He was given a form and directions to reach the blood bank. As he left, our time was also over. We had to take our lunch and rush for our afternoon lectures. The event of the day had drained us. We empathised with the doctors posted there. They had a tough job ahead. Thanking Dr Seema and also thanking our stars that we didn't need to stay there any longer, we left.

We had hardly crossed the corridor when we caught sight of the husband and his mother. The mother was scolding him badly.

'Are you stupid? Why did you agree to donate?'

'Her life is in danger, *Amma*.'

'*Arrey*, they just say that to scare you and make you donate blood for other people. It is a government hospital. It is their job to arrange blood.'

'But *Amma*...'

'Listen, your wife is doing what all women do. Nothing will happen to her. Last pregnancy also she was anaemic. What happened? Did she die?'

'Hmm.' He kept his head down.

'*Beta,* you are my only son. You are the one who earns for the family. What will happen if something goes wrong with you? The whole family will come to the road.'

He stared inside the labour room.

'Ask your wife. Even she will not let you donate blood.'

'Ok, *Amma*. I will go and talk to her.'

'Good and don't worry, I have sent a message for her family too.'

Disgust was a very mild emotion to describe what we felt.

'Can you please keep my apron? I just need to go and thrash this guy.' Raj muttered.

The others pulled him. We still needed to eat. But as we made our way to the common room, Raj hesitated.

'What's wrong?'

'My blood group is A-positive. I am going to the blood bank.'

'Come on, don't get emotional. You will miss the class.'

'It doesn't matter. I have wanted to do this since I turned 18. I think this is the perfect opportunity.'

'Even I want to.' Kavya joined him.

The sentiment was echoed by four more boys and two girls in our batch. Gone were the tantrum-prone, naughty medicos. Here were the responsible youth, citizens of the future. They left for the blood bank.

In my heart I envied them. But despite everything I couldn't join them. I suffered an intense needle phobia. My friends understood. I still didn't know my blood group. Even in the physiology class where we learned testing blood groups on our own blood, I had tested Kavya's instead of mine.

'A friend in need is a friend indeed.' I had reminded her.

Anyway, I would share the class notes with them. One good turn deserved another.

The next morning we reached the labour room, before time.

In Kamla Raja Hospital, the doctors had one more responsibility, that of taking out the blood samples. The nurses refused to do this. I don't know who started it but eventually it made the residents experts at jutting in that intravenous needle, in even the minutest and faintest of the veins.

In an overburdened and understaffed government hospital there is so much work piled up that help from any quarter is welcome. No wonder the house surgeon posted there looked relieved to see us. And we were enthusiastic about learning to put in the intravenous needle.

A boiler was there in the labour room and in a white tray that the ward *bai* gave us, we took out some glass syringes and vials.

'These are actually antibiotic vials that once used are opened, washed and kept for collecting blood samples.' The house surgeon informed us, while labelling them with the patients' names.

'You did all that by yourself?' I looked at the house surgeon, wondering.

'Who else?' She laughed.

Our eyes grew wide. Who else indeed!

'I once injured my finger opening the vial.'

We listened to her astonished.

She put some EDTA powder, an anticoagulant that prevented blood from clotting in some of the vials and said, 'Here, these are EDTA vials. You take heamogram in them. Collect blood for other tests in the plain vials.'

'No disposable syringes?' We asked.

'You can ask the ones who can afford to buy one. But sometimes they start fighting.' She replied.

Clearly, HIV was not in the list of their priorities and the hospitals were witness to much different problems.

We met Dr Seema in the corridor.

'What happened to the patient, Ma'am?' We couldn't resist asking her about the anaemic patient.

'She was transfused blood but then around midnight without telling anyone she went to the bathroom on her own. She collapsed there.'

'Oh! That's so sad.'

'It is. That's how anaemia kills. The heart is already strained with the volume overload and it suddenly gives away. I have seen many patients collapsing like this, especially when they went into labour.'

'All your efforts went in vain.' She looked at us with regret. She knew that we had donated blood.

Despite the paucity of resources we had tried our best. I thought about her husband and children.

'He has taken it badly. He looked broken.' This could have been easily prevented if they had got her checkups done in pregnancy.

'If only he had not listened to his mother. He kept on saying this over and again.' Dr Seema added.

Leaving us brooding, Dr Seema left for the labour room.

'Let's see a delivery today.' Kavya said breaking the gloom.

'Sounds good!' We had a fair idea now about the mechanism of labour. It was time for some real action now.

'Sister, can you tell us which patient is going to deliver?'

It was a right question but we were asking the wrong person. In a government hospital, nurses are not people you can mess up with, or ask questions that are beneath them, especially if they happen to be 'in-charge'. They were a force to reckon with and they wanted you to understand that, early on.

In our naivety, we had dared to ask the labour room nurse in-charge something as mundane as a patient's findings. She eyed us up and down.

'Third years?'

'Yes sister, sorry, Ma'am!' We squirmed under her gaze.

'Go and ask the doctors. You can also read the case sheets and follow the progress notes. And don't leave them here and there.' She rolled her eyes.

She pointed towards a doctor in a blue dress. Dr Neeta, as we were told, was a second-year PG who had done her MBBS from Bhopal.

Her patient was a *primigravida,* meaning it was her first pregnancy and she was in labour.

Dr Neeta was doing the vaginal examination of the patient.

Thin, blue curtains separated the labour tables affording some privacy to the patients. Just like in crowded households, privacy is something that is neither respected nor found in plenty in teaching hospitals and here it was no exception.

Doctor was a gender-neutral word and a patient, especially in a government hospital, could not choose the gender of her doctor. She could not say no to being watched by the curious eyes of medical students. A doctor's white coat gave them the right to intrude in the name of learning. But, we took lessons from them and whatever their social status, it earned them our respect. They taught us more than any textbook.

What we shared with them was much beyond the doctor-patient relationship. Their contribution in the making of a doctor was something even they themselves could never comprehend.

As we gathered around her table, she drew her sheets a little further. But, soon she was gripped by a bout of pain and twisted around. She was not howling as we had imagined a woman would in labour. Courtesy of Bollywood movies!

Dr Neeta stretched the index and middle fingers of her right hand and said, 'She is around 6 cm. Cervix is thin now about 60 percent taken up and the baby's head is at station 0.'

The fingers of a gynaecologist measured better than any scale. The distance between the two fingers, index and the middle finger, the angle between the two showed more accurately the dilatation than words.

As the patient progressed in labour, the fingers stretched wider, the angle between them more obtuse.

When the mouth of uterus or cervix thinned out and gradually merged with the rest of the uterus allowing easy passage to the baby, it was called 'taken up'.

The position of the baby was conveniently divided at stations. At the pelvic brim (inlet to the birth canal), it was station -3, as it came down it reached the ischial spines at station 0. In its descent, it kept crossing stations till it became visible at the outlet at +2.

She was having good contractions. Her foetal heartbeat was heard every 30 minutes and it was regular signalling that the baby was doing fine.

An hour later she let out a sudden scream.

'Doctor, I can feel a lot of pressure.' She complained.

The patient was fully dilated, ready for delivery. The nurse rushed, bringing the patient to the edge of the table and she was told to bear down. We could feel our heart beating faster.

And as the whole staff gathered around her chanting '*Jor laga, jor laga; push kar, push kar*'. She turned pink, panting and pushing and suddenly the baby started showing.

'Why is everybody calling for Pushkar?' Sameer winked and we all laughed. Pushkar was our immediate senior.

It was so out of the world, watching the head doing the slow descent, crowning and then gradually emerging into the material world, ending its maiden dance.

With fascination, we watched a real baby emulate the '*gudda*-pelvis' and show us in all glory the mechanism of true labour.

Soon the baby was in the hand of the doctor.

But to the horror of all present there, the baby didn't cry!

Later, I realised that this was the time our racing hearts indeed had an arrest. Dr Neeta was suddenly frantic. She cut the cord and dashed to the suction table.

'Where's the paediatrician?' Those were not the days of mobile phones. Another doctor was calling up the nursery from the landline phone.

In the meantime, Dr Neeta had put the baby head down, rubbing her back and tapping her feet. It still didn't cry. She slapped the baby.

Desperate situations, desperate measures. To our relief, the baby moved her limbs. Dr Neeta did a quick suction of the baby's mouth, cleaned the mucous and started giving oxygen. It was now three minutes to delivery and the baby had not yet cried. The Apgar score was poor.

'Thank god, the baby is pink. The heart is also doing fine. Where the hell is the paediatrician?'

'Let's start the ambu bag.' Another post-graduate had come to her aid. We could see attendants peeping from the corridor. The nurse moved to close the door.

The door was suddenly thrust open and the paediatrician rushed inside. Looking at the way he was breathing we gathered he must have run all the way.

'Why don't you people come in time?' At least ten pairs of eyes looked at him accusingly.

'Ma'am, I just received your call. And I left a sick baby in the nursery to come here.' He refused to feel guilty.

'But we had sent a written call with the ward *bai* half an hour back.'

Suddenly a shrill cry interrupted their squabble from getting serious. The baby was crying!

It was like music to our ears, more beautiful, more melodious than even a piece of Mozart. It was not only relief that reflected on the faces watching her, but also a strange tenderness. I reached out and touched the baby. It was such a beautiful feeling to touch the baby's soft skin, even if it was covered with thick, white vernix.

The paediatrician had taken charge. He shooed everyone away, wrapped up the baby and brought it near her mother.

'Look at the baby. Tell me what it is.' He exposed the baby a little to show her sex.

'Girl.' The tired mother said weakly. This was very important. The sex had to be revealed, said out aloud a couple of times, and then the footprints taken and an identity tag tied around its wrist before the baby was taken away.

'She needs to be under observation. We will have to keep her in the nursery. Your attendants are outside?' He explained to the patient.

The patient nodded.

While we were busy watching the baby, another doctor had removed the placenta.

'Now that they have told her she has a girl, she will start bleeding.' Dr Seema muttered.

'Why?'

'They go into stress. The uterus relaxes and starts bleeding. Sister, keep the oxytocin drip flowing for the next two hours.'

'I hope you are not sad.' Dr Neeta asked the patient.

'Why would anyone be sad on having such a beautiful baby?' Raj whispered. The rest of us wondered too.

'I am not, but can't say about my family, especially my mother-in-law.' The new mother looked outside worriedly.

We were reminded about this force that existed in our households, the mother-in-law.

I was the second-born girl in my family. I wondered if my parents were sad when I was born. But my *Dadi* loved me. I shrugged away the unpleasant thought.

'You should be thankful it is a girl. They are born fighters. Boys are much weaker. They wouldn't have come out of this easily.' Dr Neeta was telling her.

Girls were biologically the stronger sex at birth. Sadly things changed soon, thereafter.

'Is being a girl such a curse?' Sameer whispered. Living in our safe confines I had never realised that.

The patient was now covered and shifted to a bed.

'Congratulations!' We told her.

'Thank you.' She sounded grateful. 'I hope my baby is fine.'

We were hoping that too. But our adventure for the day had come to an end. We had to leave the labour room.

I suddenly caught Sameer gazing at the case sheet.

'This looks so cute.' He pointed towards the inked footprint of the baby.

'Fingerprints come much later in life. We don't take it because it's cute, but because it's the earliest identity proof.' Dr Neeta told us. 'Sometime back a patient had a baby girl in the labour room and another one had a baby boy by caesarean in the operation theatre. The one who had a baby girl claimed that we had swapped the babies.'

'Because they wanted a boy?' Sameer asked.

Dr Neeta shrugged. 'It turned out to be very bitter with a lot of media coverage. Since then it became mandatory to take footprints immediately after birth.'

As third years we were supposed to get just a feel of the obstetrics and gynaecology department. The more enthusiastic ones got to watch caesareans too but generally not many of us were keen at that stage to enter into the operation theatre.

We were in our second professional where the main subjects were pathology, pharmacology and forensic medicine. Here, too, obstetrics and gynaecology made its presence felt strongly and later again in community medicine as well during our final professional part I. Almost everything they taught in obstetrics and gynaecology, and paediatrics somehow made it to the national registers and were important demographic indicators, the ones that showed not only the health but also the social well-being of the country.

Soon, the labour room and all our adventures were pushed to the back of our mind as we got immersed, slogging in subjects as vast and engrossing as pathology and pharmacology and as compelling yet gut-wrenching like forensic medicine.

Final Year

'Medical schools provide perhaps the best substantiation for Charles Darwin's theory of natural selection. For here we see in its cruellest form the survival of the fittest, not the smartest, as one should expect. But the fittest to cope with the inhuman pressures, the demands made not only on the brain but on the psyche...'

—*Doctors,* Erich Segal

Not much had changed in the obstetrics and gynaecology department in the last two years. The crowded corridors, stinking bathrooms, the patients, even the teachers were the same. What had changed was the intensity of its presence in our lives. It was our main subject and focus now. Final professional was considered to be the toughest exams and a year later the mega giant, Pre-PG entrance exams, awaited us. Gynaecology was a scoring subject, relatively easier than its more difficult counterparts—medicine and surgery. Most girls could relate to the subjects but barring few who dare not show their interest, majority of the boys were still the same. They failed to fathom the hard work done in a department which had maximum emergencies, and was also the most litigant department where majority of the complications were unpredictable and mostly non-preventable. It was a department that worked 24 × 7, the surgeries never postponed, the doctors always alert and empathetic.

Still something had changed—the boys! They had become much bolder. Tuned by their seniors they knew how to unruffle the gynaecology teachers and disrupt their classes.

Our senior batch was notorious. They often carried small fire crackers into the gynae classroom. Once in the middle of the class on 'management of eclampsia', suddenly a cracker burst and everyone, including the teachers, rushed outside in panic. The guys had their quota of fun.

They even carried a small puppy inside the classroom once. The small canine found 150 pairs of eyes suddenly focussed on him and he buckled. He let out a whining sound as the chorus chanted, '*Badhai ho, apko baby hua hai* (Congratulations, you've been blessed with a baby)!' The disgusted teacher walked away!

Our theory classes were now more frequent and more gruelling. The obstetrics and gynae definition had been sorted out and so had gravidity and parity. We had moved on to more serious topics like obstetrical disorders and malpresentaions.

Dr Mahajan was a gentle lecturer. Her only problem was that she kept rearranging her saree much too often. So, even while she taught the nitty-gritties of medical termination of pregnancy (MTP), her much-too-obvious efforts belied her confidence. Her nervousness brought snorts of laughter from the class.

However, minus a little ruckus, the boys of our class were quite well behaved. They maintained discipline especially in the professor's class. She had an air and was rarely alone. The protocol surrounding her was difficult to intercept.

Dr Batra was the youngest and smartest and knew how to handle the guys. They were a little wary of troubling both of them.

It was another senior lecturer who despite her seniority faced the brunt. From disrupting her class to her alleged affair with another senior lecturer, she was talked about the most. Medical schools were notorious for their rumoured link ups. It took not more than a casual 'hello' and being spotted together that would set the rumour mongers rolling.

The class was on fibroid uterus. A very important topic yet there were few takers for that! After attendance, the class fell into a little order and Dr Bali, an excellent clinician and a good teacher, started her lecture on fibroids.

'Fibroids are benign tumours of the uterus. They are of three types: submucosal, subserosal and intramuscular.'

As she turned towards the blackboard to draw the diagrams, the back-benchers broke into a chorus: '*Kaliganj ki bahu*! *O Kaliganj ki bahu*!' That brought in a bout of laughter, obviously not from the teacher but the students.

She turned around and stared angrily at the class. 'If you don't want to study, you can go out.' She shouted to no one in particular. Nobody moved.

Promptly, everyone fell silent. But, silence in the classrooms especially that of gynaecology was rare and eerie.

It was maintained till she turned towards the blackboard again. The chorus '*Kaliganj ki bahu*' broke out once more. This was lifted from a popular TV serial of that time *Muzrim Hazir Ho*. It continued for a few more times after which Dr Bali threw a piece of chalk on the back-benchers and walked out of the class in disgust.

Rather than being scared, the class kept laughing for another ten minutes.

The idea was never to insult the teachers but just to have fun. Not something that should be emulated but probably even the teachers understood it. The medical students were as famous for their mischief as their studies.

Even the notorious seniors had all cleared their exams. Probably the department understood the futility of keeping them for another year. They were meant for other branches, not obstetrics, at least not in majority of the North Indian states. We often lamented at the unfairness of it all. No liberties were ever given in the name of the 'fairer sex' when it came to dealing with hernia, hydrocele or any parts of the male anatomy. Rather, we were dared to rise up to the challenge.

The one-hour class, thanks to the boys, was over in less than 20 minutes.

'Come on, girls, you can read everything from Shaw's. Fibroid is very well described in that book.' Sameer tried to goad us.

Not surprisingly he owed even this information to us.

'Of course, you boys don't have any intention of reading textbooks.' I said.

'I have a better idea. I can swap your answer sheet in the examination hall.' Raj grinned unashamedly.

'Your hands will break copying her. You will faint, I tell you.' Varun quipped.

We were walking out of the lecture hall when we saw one of the RSOs running towards the antenatal ward just behind the lecture theatre. Most of the batch, especially the back-benchers had disappeared to the canteen. Only a few of us were left behind. The RSO looked jittery and was in a hurry.

'Sister, do you have adrenaline?' She asked.

'No, Doctor.' The nurse replied.

'Oh my god! Where is madam?' She rushed to the HOD's office.

'What happened, Sister?' We asked the nurse.

'A patient in the Family Planning OT has suffered a cardiac arrest.'

We rushed towards the operation theatre.

Dr Batra was hovering over the door, looking shaken and drained. She looked different without her smile and her composure washed away. She passed a fleeting glance at us before turning back to the patient. We could not enter inside the operation theatre but stood outside curious to know about her.

We spotted Swati inside. She was posted in the Family Planning OT and had gone there soon after the class.

'What happened?' We surrounded her.

'She was an infertility patient and had come for a diagnostic laparoscopy.' She explained.

'Why did she have a cardiac arrest? Did she have a heart disease?'

'No.'

'It might be sensitivity to Xylocaine.' We tested the little knowledge that we had gained.

'The Xylocaine sensitivity test was done. There was no reaction. There was no known allergy either.' Swati elaborated.

'They had taken her on the table and had just given local anaesthesia when she had an arrest.'

There were so many doctors there trying to resuscitate her but she remained critical. She was soon shifted to the ICU.

A strong vagal attack or simply an unexplained cardiac arrest. Had they missed out something and were caught unawares?

'Maybe they gave the medicine IV rather than IM (intramuscular), straight to heart,' Varun said. Normally he refrained from thinking, but when he did he came up with gems like these.

'Stop watching too many Hindi movies.' I rebuked him.

The doctors were having a tough time explaining to the attendants. It was always difficult to answer when you were struggling with the question.

You can't expect people to understand an unprecedented adverse outcome. All fingers pointed at the doctors, including their own.

When you are responsible for a patient, the guilt sometimes kills in more ways than one can ever imagine.

'Nobody comes to the hospital expecting an outcome like this and when it happens the reactions are bound to be shocking.' We conceded.

'Doctors have botched it up.' The voices could be heard in the corridor.

'A healthy woman, how could she die?' It kept on bogging everyone.

The next few days saw all the wards, labour room and the operation theatres checking their crash carts. The life-saving drugs had to be there but as usual in a resources-starved hospital it was the resident's kit that remained the most bankable and equipped one to handle these emergencies. And soon in the mad turnover of patients and the emergencies, the deficiencies and even the unfortunate patient would be forgotten. The hospital would move on.

The next day we decided to explore the Family Planning OT itself.

Two anaesthetists were posted there. From giving the test dose to the local anaesthesia, they were doing it themselves.

'They were even checking the vials and breaking it themselves.' Swati spoke just loud enough for our ears, 'Till yesterday it was the gynae house surgeon doing this.'

New patients, new doctors, new attitude; it was a new day and things were getting back on track in the busy theatre.

Broadly two groups of patients could be found in the Family Planning OT—one desperate to get pregnant and the other desperate to terminate it.

'Isn't it kind of eerie that they are seated together?' I whispered to Kavya. Just how unfair God could be?

'I hope my tubes are normal.' A woman waiting for her turn spoke anxiously. 'They call me barren in my village.' She kept her eyes downcast.

They were brought to the theatre to undergo diagnostic laparoscopy. A telescope was put through a button-hole incision on her abdomen and the tubes were tested for patency.

'Tuberculosis is the main culprit, destroying her tubes and blocking her future too.' We were told.

A woman in the OT dress stood in the corner, looking very anxious.

'I have come to get my tubes re-connected, once again.'

'Why?' It sounded interesting.

'I had two children. We didn't want more so I got my sterilisation operation done. Few years back we had gone to Rishikesh. My daughter had stayed back at home. My son being the youngest was a little naughty. As we were taking a holy dip in the Ganges he sauntered off into the deep water. Suddenly we saw him being carried away by the strong currents.' She started sobbing. 'We couldn't save him. It's been two years but I can't live without him. I want him back.'

I felt sad for her.

'Tuboplasty is a good alternative for you.' I told her. Tubal recannalisation was especially good for those who couldn't afford or didn't want to go for IVF. Our professor was a very good surgeon and we sincerely hoped it worked for her.

'Best of luck! You will have him back.' I reassured her.

'Come on girls, there are many more consents to be taken.' Our senior's voice made us hurry to the next patient. There were many more case sheets to be completed.

'You are undergoing an MTP and a sterilisation together?' We asked the next patient.

'I didn't have a choice.' She made a sullen face.

'No, abortion shall be done alone. Either with a Copper-T insertion or tubal ligation. Else every few months you are going to turn up with a pregnancy.' The nurse reprimanded her.

'Unfortunately abortion is still a method of contraception to them.' She elaborated.

'If only I had a choice I would never do an MTP.' The seniors said with disdain. Yet, for both the patients and the doctor it was a compulsion.

'If you refuse you would risk sending her to a quack and to septic abortion later on. Unsafe abortion is the leading yet the most easily preventable cause of maternal death!' Our senior explained.

But was it really a woman's choice?

'Why not male sterilisation?' We asked the RSO posted there.

'Let me show you.' She said sarcastically.

'Why doesn't your husband undergo sterilisation?' She asked the next patient.

'*Hamara aadmi akela kamata hai, woh kaise jayega operation karane* (My husband is the sole earner, how can he get operated)?' She promptly replied.

With two previous caesareans, she was willing to go under the knife a third time but would not let her husband have the surgery.

'But it is a much simpler surgery.' Our senior tried to convince her.

'*Nahi,* Madam. *Operation se usko kamzori aa jayegi* (No, Madam, the operation will make him weak).' There were lot of misconceptions, the fear of impotency leading the list.

Female sterilisation too struggled with prejudices.

'We don't have anyone at home. How will we rest after the operation?' Groaned one reluctant acceptor.

'You lose so much blood during abortion. On the contrary there is hardly any loss of blood during ligation yet there is so much bias against it.' The resident was shaking her head.

'*Arrey* Ma'am, if you leave it to them they will come for multiple abortions every year without a single day of rest.' The nurse complained.

'Madam, *hamari bhabhi ki Copper-T upar chadh gayi thi* (Madam, my sister-in-law's Copper-T was pushed above).'

'It has got no hand and feet. How can it freely roam in the body?' The nurse defended. 'A moving baby stayed inside the uterus but the Copper-T moved!'

It was difficult to see logic when popular hearsays took precedence.

'I gained weight after Copper-T. It made me so fat that I had to get it removed.' Another one, waiting for an abortion added.

There were cases where it did get displaced but then those were rare and blown out of proportion.

Meanwhile, the seniors were all caught up in a different kind of emergency.

The patient was an unmarried girl around five months pregnant and had reported to the casualty with a strange problem.

'By the time I realised I was pregnant it was already beyond four months.' She admitted.

'My boyfriend took me to a doctor. They gave me a medicine and soon shifted me into the operation theatre to clean my uterus.'

'In India it isn't legal to terminate beyond 20 weeks. She might have visited a quack or maybe an overzealous doctor keen to help an unmarried girl! Sometimes doctors too get carried away.' The resident posted there explained.

'I kept on bleeding so they thought that the abortion was not complete and took me inside the theatre again. But this time they got suspicious and referred me.' The girl said.

She arrived here with her bowel hanging outside her vagina and a stench covering her. A diagnosis of perforation of the uterus was made. Termination so late in pregnancy was fraught with dangers.

'If they are smart to be in a relationship, they should be smart enough to learn about contraception and abortion too.' Our professor said disapprovingly, as she cut through the layers exposing her bowel and uterus.

We watched fascinated.

'Call the surgeon. Her bowel has been injured.' She looked up, worried.

Dr Deepak, our professor in surgery arrived. He took a few minutes to explore her intestines and informed, 'Her small intestine needs to be removed.' There was no choice and he went on to complete the surgery. The poor girl's future minus her bowels loomed ahead..

Her parents had also arrived and as we moved outside we saw them waiting with anxious faces. The boyfriend also sat there, his head bowed.

'He looks brave.' Kavya was staring at him.

'He didn't run away.' I agreed.

'Is she going to be alright?' Her parents stood with folded hands. The poor people were hardly aware of all that was going through their daughter's life.

We avoided answering them and moved out.

We walked inside the labour room after a hiatus of two years and were immediately taken in by the dynamism and hectic movement there.

Something was going on inside. The patient had been brought to the edge of the table and her legs tied in stirrups. She was groaning and twisting in pain. A table was neatly set alongside her bed. On it lay long, grotesque instruments. The mere look was intimidating. What were they up to?

The patient was referred from a village with intrauterine death of baby. She was now in active labour, fully dilated but the baby was stuck.

Destructive surgery was a lost art. Very few were now trained to do it. Yet in a developing country like ours, a safely performed destructive surgery in the setting of a dead baby saved the patient from surgery.

This was not a frequently performed procedure and it was evident by the number of doctors surrounding her.

'Take a stool and stand on it. You will be able to watch better.' The labour room nurse advised me. It was a good idea.

I fortunately found some space to stand behind Dr Bali and watched her.

'First, empty her bladder. Then guarding the blades put this perforator inside. Seema, will you please keep the head stable from above?'

Dr Seema held the head as in first pelvic grip.

'Now, under the guidance of the fingers of my left hand I slowly introduce this perforator till it reaches the head of the foetus. Open it so that it makes a deep cut in the skull. Then again withdraw it a little. Now, rotate the blade and make another cut. You can now see a cross-shaped incision. Then withdraw the perforator.'

She placed it back on the table.

'Let's now put this Budin's cannula inside the skull and churn out the brain matter. The idea is to make the skull collapse so that it can be extracted out.' A nauseating smell was filling my senses. This was nothing short of butchery. I debated whether I should move out but felt that would look thoroughly unprofessional. I closed my eyes.

'Let's now insert the cranioclast.' I briefly opened my eyes to see Dr Bali pointing at the horrific-looking blade. I reminded myself for the umpteenth time that the baby was dead inside.

'The solid blade is to be inserted inside the skull through the earlier incision that we made. The fenestrated blade shall go behind the skull guided by the fingers placed internally so that you don't injure any other structure. Now, lock the instrument. The skull is now firmly in the grip of the two blades. You can now pull out the baby like you do with the forceps.'

A large thud behind me forced me to open my eyes. The smell was now suffocating. I saw the macerated stillborn baby lying on the table still in the grip of the two blades of the instrument. The sight was as revolting as the smell. But the sound? It had come from behind.

I moved behind to see the stool tumbled and Raj sprawled on the floor. The chicken-hearted medico! Not that I blamed him.

He woke up after being shaken a few times. We took him out.

'Here, have some water.' Dr Bali had come out to see him. She looked at him gently.

'Life is not easy, son. It is so easy to create a ruckus in the class. Try doing this sometimes.' She smiled. There was no vanity in her voice and we felt a trifle ashamed.

'Sometimes you have to do something ugly just to ensure that the future of the patient remains beautiful. Now it's over and tomorrow she might go home too. That's the beauty of vaginal delivery. Always remember that. She will carry no scar, neither on her uterus, nor her skin nor on her obstetric future.'

Dr Bali that day had done something which was unique and beautiful. But one that I would never attempt. It was an art that would truly die with my brilliant teacher and we would carry on the blame of increasing the caesarean section rate. Not a single person I know from that lot could ever emulate that feat.

A few days later I saw her doing decapitation in another dead foetus that was stuck. But this time we neither felt nauseated nor passed out. Rather we watched in reverence as she pulled out the brilliant feat.

Medical college was also the time for getting fascinated by your seniors, usually the postgraduates. The gynaecology department held no fascination for us girls. It was the other departments especially surgery and orthopaedics which bore the brunt of our crushes. There was not much future in these fascinations. It rarely went beyond a few classes but then they were the most exciting times, attending the clinical postings while drooling like besotted fools, even if you were not alone in that!

Swati and Payal were on the way to the hospital when they were told about the scooter of their latest 'crush' parked in front of the JA Hospital. This building housed the medical and surgical wards of male patients, along with some hunks, the hot residents, the talk of the town!

Every other plan for the day was stalled there, indefinitely.

We left them there and proceeded for our very own gynaecology postings.

It was around 5 pm when we entered the labour room emergency. The residents were on their evening tea break. There were a few patients in early labour and none about to deliver. We waited for them to finish tea and requested for something that was on our mind for a long time.

'Ma'am, we want to do a PV.' We requested.

PV meant a per-vaginal examination.

'Oh okay.'

Those were the days of reused gloves. Even the disposable ones were washed, powdered, sterilised and reused.

We took one out tentatively. The first lesson was of wearing the gloves the right way, maintaining asepsis. It wasn't easy. We struggled as we tried to make sense of where our thumb should go. With much difficulty we managed to wear our gloves.

'Lock both your hands together. You cannot touch anything now.' Our senior advised us.

'Else you become sterile.' Varun was busy pulling Raj's leg.

'First, you stop putting so much powder on your face.' Raj wasn't the one to take it lying down. He had once caught Varun doing exactly that, just before he entered the dissection hall in the first year.

'Ask the patient to empty her bladder. Then explain to her what you are doing. That will relax her.' The duty doctor explained to us.

The RSO put her fingers inside and asked us to feel the cervix, the mouth of the uterus.

I stood for my turn. As I introduced my index and middle fingers inside, all I could feel was warm flesh closing on my fingers. My insides clenched. I could barely feel anything else and before I could reach the cervix I felt dizzy. My head swam and I took off my gloves to sit at the bench.

'What happened?' The RSO looked concerned.

'I don't know. I felt giddy.'

I realised later that it was a vagal response, a syncopal attack. Many of us students had it right from the first time in the dissection hall to witnessing the first surgery.

I had always prided myself on being strong. Well, pride hath a fall. At least I had prevented the drama of falling down.

'You take rest and do it some other time.' She reassured me. I nodded, sure in my heart there would never be a next time. Little did I know that destiny was already making different plans for me.

Suddenly Dr Vidya, a beautiful RSO, entered the labour room. 'Can you please send a "call" to the medicine RMO on duty?' She spoke a little breathlessly.

A call was a letter that was sent to any other department if you wanted the other speciality to come and see your patient.

'Please write "To the RMO on duty, Patient Bala Devi, 35 years, female, bed no. 5, post-natal ward is suffering from severe *ghabrahat* (anxiety) and breathlessness. Please come and see her urgently.'

A meaningful glance passed between the two RSOs, one which I failed to intercept. It was already 8 pm and I didn't want to goof up again. I felt proud of my legible handwriting and gave it to the ward *bai,* to take it to the medical ward.

An hour later two guys entered our labour room from the medicine department.

'There was an urgent call.' They showed the call, that slip of paper.

'You are on duty?' Dr Vidya's eyes rolled upwards, surprised.

'Actually, Dr Lokesh is on duty. But he was busy so he requested us to go and see the patient.' They explained.

I could see Dr Vidya didn't like that.

'Where is the post-natal ward?' They asked.

These guys were new to the hospital.

'Can you please take them there?' Dr Vidya looked at me.

I took them to the post-natal ward. However, bed no. 5 was empty. There was no patient lying there. As we looked around, another one called out her name. Bala Devi walked inside holding her baby in her arms.

'What is your problem?' The medicine RMO asked.

She looked at them blankly.

'Aren't you having *ghabrahat* and breathlessness?' He asked again.

'I delivered last night. Was having some indigestion probably but *ghabrahat*...' her voice trailed off.

'Are you Bala Devi?' I asked.

'Of course.' The lady said.

He took out her case sheet and wrote: 'Patient presently having no medical complaints. Continue same treatment.' They handed me the case file and left. As I followed them I could overhear them saying, 'This has become a routine whenever Dr Lokesh is on duty. That's why he sent us today.'

We were not alone in our infatuations! This was hilarious. So much went into those corridors, much beyond medicine. After all, doctors were human too, plagued by the same emotions.

I rushed back to the labour room. Dr Vidya was nowhere to be seen. As I looked around for her I was stopped by a woman.

'Sister, can you check the baby?'

I peered at the baby. It was carefully bundled in a torn blanket. I was in a hurry to find Dr Vidya and tell her about the patient and Dr Lokesh.

'What happened?' I asked.

'The baby has passed urine.'

I stared at her. What was I supposed to do with that? She caught me staring at her and flushed.

'Actually…they had told me it was dead!'

I was shocked.

'My daughter delivered an hour ago. Tell me how can it pass urine if it is dead?'

I struggled to answer. To my relief Dr Vidya turned up and found me talking to the woman.

'Why don't you people understand? First you bring her late. She was not perceiving foetal movements for two days. But you kept her at home.'

She lowered her head.

'And, now when we tell you the baby is dead you don't believe us.' Dr Vidya sounded exasperated. 'We showed you the dead baby on ultrasound too.'

'But my daughter said she had felt some movement during labour pains.'

'There was no heart beat. She must have felt the bowel movements.'

'Then why would the baby pass urine?' The woman insisted.

'The paediatrician explained this to you too.'

The woman then went to the nursery to see the paediatrician again.

'The baby goes into rigor mortis and sometimes muscles contract expelling some amount of urine.' The paediatrician had explained and just for her satisfaction examined the baby again and declared it dead.

She still kept the bundle close to her heart.

Sighing, Dr Vidya moved inside. I peered outside. The poor woman was sitting in the corridor clutching the bundle and staring in the dark. I wondered if she had anyone with her.

Her daughter, exhausted from the delivery, slept on the labour table. These were the times when you felt so helpless. Each one of them who laboured, breathed their own story, some happy, some tragic; some crowded and some alone.

A villager had travelled a long distance to reach the hospital. He stood waiting in the examination room adjoining the labour room. This also served as gynae casualty. Not all patients who came here had an emergency. Some came simply because the time suited them. A hospital couldn't refuse seeing even a 'routine' patient in emergency. They didn't bother straining the already stretched emergency staff.

But then I really wondered what troubled him. He was an old man and was accompanied by a young girl around 20, who hid behind him.

'What happened?' I asked.

'She's my daughter-in-law.' He hesitated for a while and then continued. 'She got married to my son about two years back. But then they have not been married in the true sense till now.'

'Where is her husband?' It was out before I could stop myself.

'*Ghar ke bade hain* (We are the elders). We are the ones who have to take them to hospital. He was busy with his work.'

I took the girl inside.

'Do you have periods?'

She kept quiet.

'What was your last date?'

'I've never had menses.' Her quiet voice shocked me.

'Not even once?' Was she primary amenorrhea, meaning she never had menses even once? I peered at her with curiosity. Still a novice in gynae, I was thinking more like any other non-medical person.

Dr Vidya was back. She made the girl lie on the examination table and after examining her, concluded, 'She has a blind vagina.' Oh the *mullerian agenesis*! I had read about this in embryology. No uterus tubes and absent vagina.

In her case, there was a small dimple where the vagina should have ideally existed. She must have known about this before her marriage too.

'Usually they come to know about it when they don't have their menses. But then most of them will hide it because of social stigma.'

'But isn't it treatable?'

'They don't come to the hospitals fearing the worst. If they have a uterus then the prognosis is better. Otherwise it gets difficult.'

'But if they have a uterus, won't they menstruate?'

'Sometimes the uterus may be underdeveloped too and they don't menstruate. It's the ones who do, that need urgent treatment!' Dr Vidya continued, 'You must see this girl admitted in the post-operative ward who kept on having cyclical pain but no menstruation. The uterus would get full of blood every month but won't drain out. She had an imperforate hymen. A simple cut on the hymen relieved all her agony.'

Reading about a condition was one thing, but seeing a practical case was such an enlightening experience.

'We keep seeing such patients of blind vagina. Some are partial and some complete.'

'But then her husband would have found out soon after marriage?' We were curious about the one sitting in front of us. She was married for two years.

'You will be surprised by the level of knowledge people have. Let's ask her.'

'I was not having menses but my mother asked me to keep quiet. I didn't know that there was something seriously wrong with me.' The girl spoke softly.

'And your husband?'

She hesitated. 'We thought most couples have these problems. Even he was a novice and didn't understand much.

But lately he had started getting doubtful. Moreover, I was not conceiving, so he talked to his parents.'

It was still weird that her father-in-law was the one to have brought her here. Different circumstances, different lives. It was not a good thing to be judgemental.

Suddenly she started sobbing. The impact of having been born without a vagina was hitting her now.

'Will they now throw me out? Please don't tell my father-in-law.'

It wasn't easy. They had a right to know.

'You can be treated. You can go home now. Get these tests done and come to the outdoor clinic.' Dr Vidya wrote some test for her.

She explained everything to her father-in-law. They then thanked us and left.

'I hope she has a uterus and ovaries. Her other sexual characters look fine, though.' Dr Vidya mused.

Our eyes went round. This was getting interesting. Was she thinking about intersex too?

'I have a feeling she's not. But we shall have to look at that angle too.'

Strangely, the incidence of intersex was not as high as the ones we saw on the traffic signals. Most of them were transvestites.

'Even if she has no uterus and ovaries, she might not be able to conceive but still lead a normal life. There's even a non-surgical method using dilators. Anyway, the vagina can be created surgically. Our professor does very good vaginoplasty.'

We kept our fingers crossed.

'The results are best when the treatment is started around the time of marriage. But then some people breathe easier living in ignorance.'

It was all getting confusing now and we mentally resolved to read the textbooks again.

'Wait till you see the double uterus and the double vagina.' Dr Vidya laughed intercepting our dazzled looks. It sounded so interesting.

We had hardly moved out into the duty room when we heard a lot of noise coming from the labour room.

Someone was shouting at the doctors.

'I will not have a caesarean at any cost.' He was pointing a rude finger at the doctors there.

'The baby is in transverse lie. It is of good weight, a healthy baby. There is no way she can deliver vaginally.' Dr Vidya warned him.

'I will take her home.' He was not ready to listen.

'*Bachcha arra hai, bhaiyya. Phas jayega* (The baby is lying transversely. It will get obstructed).' She repeated.

In cases like these, the patient could go into obstructed labour and rupture her uterus. The baby could die and so could she.

Nonetheless, the husband loomed dangerously over the doctors. The nurses had also come to the defence of the doctors. The other postgraduates soon called the hostel from the landline. By that time the security guard had arrived, too.

'*Bhaiyya,* you sign here that you are leaving against the medical advice.' The nurse interrupted him.

'I will not sign anything.' He threatened. Four heavily built men crept closer to him.

These were the times you were reminded about the absent security system in the hospital. The ancient walls, creaking doors and windows, the meek security guards with just a thick, wooden rod was all that stood between the doctor and the angry attendants. If nothing went wrong that day we were thankful to the attendants, not our security system.

He just dragged his wife out of the labour room and left, without signing a single paper. We could do nothing to stop them.

'Fanatics! I shall move to the UK after my MBBS.' Raj muttered.

'Madam*ji,* I hope he doesn't come back tomorrow with a baby, just like that other patient.' The nurse said and then went on to tell us about another patient whose husband had taken her away and she ended up having a normal delivery at home. Obviously by a *dai*!

'Why couldn't we?' I wondered.

'We can never resort to unscientific methods. Nobody will spare you if things go wrong.' The other RSO replied firmly.

The rowdy husband did come back. Not with a baby, but with the patient and one 'blue' hand hanging outside her vagina and the cord prolapsed outside. It was a reminder of how things had turned out dreadfully wrong. The baby was dead. And the patient was now a case of 'rupture uterus with hand and cord prolapse of the baby'.

The tender marks on her abdomen were a sign of her night-long unsuccessful trial. Somebody must have tried to push from above causing the bruises. She looked dehydrated and tired too.

'You can never be vindictive with the patients. You have to empathise with them.' The RSO said.

The husband kept his head bowed down and stayed outside. It was the mother-in-law who stayed inside with her hand folded.

'Please forgive my son. Save my daughter-in-law.'

'Whatever his compulsions, at least he brought her back. Some don't and some came back too late.' Dr Vidya quipped.

'Women were dying, not because of diseases we cannot treat but because the society has yet to make a decision that their lives are worth saving.' I remembered this famous quote by the *Federation of International Gynaecologists and Obstetricians* (FIGO) president Mahmud Fathalla.

The patient underwent surgery and survived but without her baby and her uterus. In his obsession for a normal delivery her husband had ended up sacrificing his baby's life and the wife's uterus. The fallout left his future bleak too. He would suffer childless.

The two post-natal wards stood opposite each other. The resident posted there had the additional responsibility of making the discharges for those undergoing family planning procedures. These were the tricky ones. They had to be legible, in clear and good language. These were the ones who got incentives both financial as well as otherwise. The patients were like VIPs. After all they had done the nation a favour. No wonder they were demanding too!

Post delivery was the also the best time to motivate patients for sterilisation or contraception. The chances of acceptance were highest, fatigued as they were after their delivery. The ones who agreed were shifted to the OT the very next day of delivery.

'What is she holding in her hands?' Kavya was pointing towards the doctor.

'This is a Delta-T. It was actually a Copper-T that had the chromic catgut, a suture winded over its horizontal limb.' The RSO explained. We looked with wonder at this strange delta-shaped device.

'What's the big deal?'

'There are less chances of expulsion which otherwise happens in a rapidly involuting uterus after delivery.' Once a patient agreed it could be easily put inside before her discharge.

'There are some who never agree for either sterilisation or any contraception despite multiple deliveries. We are left with just one way to prevent their almost yearly visits.'

'So in those who have completed their family, just put this Delta-T inside, on the labour table itself.' The RSO announced.

'A "delta" drawn on their discharge summary was the only sign they carried about the intrauterine device. Their husbands didn't know about it and sometimes not even the patient.' We listened dumbstruck.

Desperate situations, desperate solutions!

A hospital that had anywhere close to 30–40 normal deliveries per day was reflected in the post-natal ward. The rounds, the dressings, the discharges; there was plenty of work piled up there.

But oblivious to all, the resident doctor was busy chatting with her friend. He was a resident in the medicine department and was posted in the female medical ward in the same building. Obviously, the two enjoyed a great affinity because it was not a good time or place to chat.

Kavya and I were the only ones in the ward that day. The post-natal ward being the last in the list of priority of all the students.

As we inched closer, she raised her head from the deep conversation she was having. She looked happy to see us there.

'Take the vitals of all the patients and start writing in the progress notes.' Obviously, that would give her more time with her friend.

She then gave us a list. 'These are the ones with episiotomy. Once you are done with the vitals, start calling the patients for dressing.' That sounded more interesting.

Handing us the BP instrument she once again started talking with the guy. We took turns in taking the vitals and jotting them down in the case sheets. We were half way through, when we noticed the next patient was sleeping. We called her out.

'Radha Rani, turn this side.' She didn't move.

'Are you alright?' Concerned we turned her. To our surprise she didn't respond. We called out to the resident.

At that very moment the professor walked inside. She marched straight to the bed, taking note of the resident engrossed in talking to her friend.

'What happened?' She looked at the patient, turned down her blanket and to our horror found her lying in a pool of blood. She reached out to feel her pulse.

'No pulse, no BP.' The professor looked obliquely at the resident. The patient was in what we medically called shock! Though it was debatable who was going to be more shocked, the professor or the resident.

Those accompanying the professor were quick to task.

'The ABC of shock management! Maintain airway, breathing and circulation.' I remembered my textbooks.

'Start the IV line quick, keep it high and let it go fast.' The professor shouted.

Within minutes the IV line was started. I looked with wonder at the ease with which the doctor accompanying the HOD had the venflon inside despite her collapsed veins. She squeezed the fluid bottle, keeping it high so that it went very fast.

'Keep massaging the uterus,' the professor instructed next.

The other one by that time had removed a large number of clots from inside the uterus adding a considerable amount to the pool of blood that was accumulating there. And with her other hand she was slowly rubbing on the uterus to bring on more contraction and reduce bleeding.

A Foley's catheter draining clear urine was put in place. We then rushed outside to help the ward *bai* bring in the stretcher. It all happened very fast.

'Ask somebody to take her samples to the blood bank and arrange blood fast.' The nurse was sending a ward *bai* along with the attendants. 'We need to replace the lost blood.' The Professor said.

She was shifted to the labour room and by that time around 1 litre of fluid had already gone.

I tentatively reached out to feel her pulse and almost erupted with joy when I could feel it. She was gaining strength and in another ten minutes she responded to our verbal command and opened her eyes. Big, dark and deep!

I had never seen more beautiful eyes and they glistened with something that was so magically iridescent. Yes, we call it life!

Shock was not just finding your professor walk into your ward when you were talking to your boyfriend, shock was when you had no palpable pulse and no recordable BP—that was a nightmare.

'Good job, girls.' The professor came to pat our back. We blushed for we had hardly done anything.

'Post-partum haemorrhage can happen to any patient. She had gone into shock, but it was still reversible.

It takes a fraction of time before they go into that grey zone of no return. The idea is to catch them before that time and that's what you girls did. It is very important to be vigilant in gynaecology wards. Things can go wrong without warning here.' She went on praising us.

We tried hard but couldn't stop our beaming pleasure. We never realised how beautiful this feeling would be, this intense feeling of saving lives. It was most liberating. It gave us a 'high' for many more days to come, something which we didn't fail to tell everyone.

The clinical postings were in full swing. Exams were drawing near very fast. There were classes on 'instruments', specimens and case presentations.

The instruments that were generally asked about were those used in MTP, the suction cannula, the MR syringe, the forceps and the vacuum. As I held the outlet forceps in my hand, I remembered my cousin who was mentally challenged. I was told that he had a forceps delivery. I turned the steel instrument in my hands. My textbook read, 'They were a steel cage that protected the head of the foetus.' It was always an emergency procedure meant to save a baby. Then why? It still troubled me. I had seen his struggle along with that of the whole family. I kept it away.

Sameer was still fiddling with it. He suddenly held it in his hands and closed the two blades on his head.

'What are you doing?' I stood horrified.

'It hurts. Just because the baby cannot give his consent do we have to subject it to torture?'

Ill equipped with the practical aspects of obstetrics we still behaved and thought like non-medical people. Hovering between knowledge and ignorance, myths and realities we were still waiting to be converted.

'If we start thinking like that we will not allow any baby to take up the journey called labour.' Dr Divya, the final-year PG who was going to take the class had silently walked inside.

'Is that why the baby cries after delivery?' We wondered. 'Was it not just to inflate the lungs?'

'Our textbooks don't teach philosophy. It's all about scientific, evidence-based facts,' she said.

'We use only outlet forceps in modern obstetrics. The head has to be at the pelvic outlet and cervix fully dilated, else you cannot use it.' This was to prevent injury to both the mother and baby.

'We use it when the mother cannot bear down or sometimes when we cannot allow her to bear as in patients with a heart disease and eclampsia. We need to cut down labour.'

She went out to demonstrate it on a foetal skull. The skull was kept inside the pelvis. Dr Divya taught us how to hold the forceps in our hands, identifying the right and left blade. Then guided safely by her fingers she applied it on both sides of the foetal head and locked it beautifully over the foetus.

'The right blade before the left and then lock. If it didn't lock easily, don't rush. It means either the foetal position is wrong or you have wrongly applied.' She instructed us.

So was it another myth that forceps could cause harm?

'If properly applied and locked, it doesn't harm the baby.' The superficial injuries heal.

'We should believe in scientific facts. Forceps are applied only when needed. They are life saving when you are not left with any other choice. Any unintentional shortcoming of the procedure has to be borne. Sometimes you are stuck and caesarean section is not always feasible.'

I told her about my cousin and the supposed injury he had suffered during childbirth.

'We are doctors, not butchers. Why would we hold a blade in one hand and hit the foetus on its head? The baby might have been already compromised. It might have buckled under some pre-existing stress during pregnancy. Do you have any idea about that?'

I shook my head. But truth was dawning on me. My aunt was a poorly controlled diabetic and he was a big-size baby. How conveniently we forget everything else and blame everything on the birthing only.

'Exactly.' She echoed my thoughts. 'We put everything upon the obstetrician.'

One mind block cleared. I looked with respect at the pair of forceps.

Another instrument we saw with interest was the 'vacuum'. This was again used to pull the foetus in desperate situations. A suction cup was applied over the foetal head and it was pulled out. The foetus generally carried a 'chignon', a swelling over the head for a few days.

Looked with suspicion, assisted vaginal delivery, as forceps and vacuum were called, were going down. Nobody was keen to take risks. This hesitancy again was one of the main reasons for the rising caesarean section rates.

Caesarean section held a lot of intrigue. We, a bunch of enthusiastic final years, peered cautiously inside the operation theatre. The nurse had very sternly asked us to change our clothes and wear a gown.

'We actually look very funny.' Sameer said looking at our oversized garb.

But it did give us a little confidence. Steering clear of the nursing in-charge, we ventured into our adventure. The nursing staff always gave us jitters. I didn't quite understand them. They looked at us tolerantly. We were final-year students, the senior most in our college. Shouldn't they treat us with lot more respect?

'Hey, listen. Don't touch everywhere that you go.' There, she shouted at us again.

'The table and all the drapes are sterilised. If you touch them, the nurse will have to bring another set. We do not always have a lot of spare stuff and thanks to your madams we have three more emergency caesareans lined up.' This grumbling doctor in green overalls was the anaesthetist, as we found out.

We tried to walk as carefully as possible. The whole atmosphere was so very intimidating.

Finally, we could manage a stool to stand upon and take a closer look at the patient. She was all draped up, surrounded by the doctors on both sides. While we watched the hands of the surgeon deftly cut through the layers of her abdomen and the uterus, we could see the head! The surgeon scooped the head in her hands and asked someone to push from above.

'Please give some fundal.' This meant a pressure to be given from the top of her tummy to push the baby down on her hands. The anaesthetist rose from his chair and obliged. Suddenly there was a cry. The baby was out. While the cord was cut and the baby taken away by the paediatrician, suddenly the operating field got all obscured. There was blood gushing from everywhere. I had never seen so much blood in my life. My head swayed.

I hurriedly got down from the stool and rushed out of the theatre. And as luck would have it, I literally bumped into the nursing in-charge.

'What happened? I hope you are okay.' She asked.

'The patient is bleeding so much.'

'Oh, is it?' She looked at the patient and then at the nurse assisting the surgery. She shook her head.

'This is how a caesarean is done, Doctor. What will you do if you were the operating surgeon? Run away?' I could see that she was mocking me.

How was I to know that a caesarean was such a bloody operation? As a final-year student I had only read about it in the textbooks.

'In a rural hospital even an MBBS should be competent to perform this surgery.' The nurse added sarcastically.

I promised myself I would never be caught in such a situation. This was definitely not my cup of tea.

Destiny as they say is always busy making plans for you, at times different and at times weird too.

The *gudda*-pelvis was back. We spent hours practicing mechanism of labour on it. The beauty of the foetus, twisting-untwisting its neck and then again twisting-untwisting its body as it negotiated the canal, fascinated us.

It was unpardonable if we goofed up. The boys still got a royal welcome while we buckled under the pressure that tilted heavily towards us.

Today, the *gudda* lay upside down in the pelvis. Well, this was 'breech' presentation, the most common of all the malpresentations. It was also called '*ulta*' in the local lingo.

'You must have been born like this.' Varun took a dig at Kavya.

The foetus could flex its buttocks, dip its footlings below or take them above its head.

'How does it really matter, heads first or tail?' One of the back-benchers quipped.

It did matter in many ways. The most serious being the aftercoming head as it was called getting stuck and then it was a no win situation. No wonder most people ended up having a planned caesarean, just to avoid this.

Yet, it was prudent to know the way out and deliver them vaginally. As our RSO went on to demonstrate how to take out the limbs slowly, one by one, then turning the trunk to allow the delivery of shoulders and then pull it down till the nape of the neck was visible and then she gradually took it over the maternal abdomen, releasing the face and…the baby was born. Looked easy enough!

You have to allow yourself flexion or the ability to bend. Just as in life! Whatever the position, the more bent or flexed the foetus was, smaller were the diameters that came out and better the chances of a safe and less-traumatic delivery.

'The foetus can't extend its head or else it becomes brow presentation, face presentation and finally chin presentation.' The RSO kept on extending the head of foetus to demonstrate the different presenting parts.

'Can you seriously feel the face of the baby?' Raj shook his face in disbelief.

'You can feel the lips, eyes, nose everything.' She smiled. 'But when you do, they are in malpresentation and generally land up in caesarean section.'

Our obstetric postings were coming to an end.

We took turns in case presentations. As final-year students, we were expected to be very good at history taking and examination. Management was important but still we were treated with kids' gloves. Theoretical knowledge was all that was expected of final years. Practicals came much later.

Contraceptives were another thing that kept us on our toes.

Varun looked worriedly at them.

'Listen.' He prodded gently. 'Why should condoms have a pearl index?'

Pearl index was the number of contraceptive failures measured in terms of duration of use by women.

'Because you need to see how effective a contraceptive method it was?' I answered. His queries generally went way above my comprehension.

'But why should we measure in terms of women's duration of use.' He persisted.

I stared at him.

'It's used by men, *na*.' He added.

There, he had done it again.

Out of the box thinking! He was definitely a thinker!

The labour room was unusually noisy today. It was almost like a weekly market. The rainy season marked the beginning of not just the downpour but deliveries too. And, the havoc it created on our already stretched medical system was beyond comprehension.

The labour tables were full. The ones in the early stages were sent to the wards. But some chose to sit in the corridors instead with their family members. They always encouraged the parturient to be mobile unlike their lazier and more lethargic urban counterparts. And more than often they came out successfully with a vaginal delivery.

But then was it always their choice or for that matter their obstetrician's either?

'The power, the passage and the passenger! The trio need to be in perfect harmony and synergy for a normal delivery.' The voice of our professor echoed in my head.

'Plus the "fundal pressure" given from above.' Our senior had winked.

It was common knowledge that though unofficial, majority deliveries owed much to this practice of a push given from above. Many nurses and ward *bais* prided themselves on their mastery over this 'art' and they were often the most sought after.

Meanwhile, the harassed-looking doctors were trying to bring some order into the chaotic labour room when a long wail cut through. Everyone looked around. Not from the labour tables, it was coming from the corner.

'The bathroom,' the labour room nurse shrugged her shoulder in resignation.

She had just come back from the scooter parking. A woman had delivered in an autorickshaw. She had rushed out with the instruments, separated the baby and had barely shifted the mother on a stretcher to the labour room. Now this!

A nurse and a ward *bai* went inside the bathroom. The patient was squatting on the Indian-style toilet when she pushed out the baby instead. The baby was brought to the labour room, cleaned and handed over to the paediatrician for ruling out any fractures. It was crying, fortunately!

The patient was shifted to the labour table.

'Remember the one who threw up a convulsion in the bathroom. It was such a pain bringing her out.' One of the resident doctors recalled.

'She has small perineal tears. Nothing serious though.' The doctor examining the patient said.

'Would any one of you want to remove the placenta?' She asked.

This sounded exciting. I clumsily donned on my gloves and stood in front of the patient. She looked tired after her expedition to the bathroom. This was the third stage of labour, after delivery. The placenta and the membranes had to be taken out.

'Keep the oxytocin running, Sister.' The doctor told the nurse. She moved on to the other patient while the nurse stood alongside me.

'Keep your left hand on her tummy and try to rub on her uterus to bring upon a contraction.' The nurse told me.

I ignored her and tried to pull the cord a little. Nothing happened.

'Madam, don't pull the cord. The placenta has not separated. You will break the cord.'

I fumed. I had read the methods of separation. Okay, I was new here but not everything was lost on me. The Brandt-Andrews method! She started gently rubbing the uterus with one hand kept on the abdomen.

'You must first watch for the signs of separation of the placenta. A fresh gush of bleeding is the first. Then put your hand just above the pubic symphysis. Above the hairline, here!' She proceeded on to show me. 'Now, start pushing it upwards and gently pull the cord down.'

The placenta had separated. It showed Mathew Duncan's method of marginal separation rather than the central Schultze method. How it chose so efficiently one of the methods! The patient groaned a little and while I gently twisted the cord and kept pulling it, it was suddenly on my hands along with the membranes.

I marvelled at the beauty and perfection of nature.

'Not always, sometimes it flips and the patient has to be taken for manual removal of placenta under anaesthesia.' My senior had come to stand beside me.

'Phew!' Whatever, that was it! I was more relieved than the patient. My first practical lesson, that too supervised by a nurse!

There was this sense of exhilaration. Yet, all I could manage was, 'Thank you, Sister,' politely to the nurse.

She smiled.

'Thank you is not enough. This calls for a samosa party.' My senior said.

The other doctors had got their '*bakra*' for the day. Well, I did feel like celebrating. I smiled sheepishly. Tea and samosas were ordered.

We were actually hungry and had hardly taken a sip of our hot tea and a bite into the tasty samosa when we were greeted by another visitor.

A feline ran out of the bathroom with her prized possession.

'Look there.'

'Yuck!' I almost spilled my tea.

She stood on the window proudly displaying her catch—the placenta! Obviously, we were not the only ones hungry here.

The ward *bai* ran after it but the cat was clever and faster too. It disappeared.

'Leave it, Rama *bai*.' The nurse laughed.

These were the cats that had grown up in the hospital. The placenta was their favourite food. The blood-rich placenta that had sustained life for months didn't go waste but was devoured hungrily by the cats. Ecofriendly disposal of waste!

The labour room taught us a lot and reached out to many more, beyond boundaries. Amniotic membranes were not redundant even after delivery. They were sometimes used as grafts to trigger healing in large wounds.

The girl with an absent vagina who had come with her father-in-law had undergone vaginoplasty and had used the amnion graft over her newly created vagina.

Nature had unknown dimensions and we were increasingly uncovering amazing facets hidden in its realms during our study.

A hospital is the best place to realise how dramatically a physiological change can get pathological. Eclampsia was one such complication, an end result of high blood pressure in pregnancy complicated by convulsions.

We were taught, 'No pregnancy should be allowed to stretch till a point where one landed up with eclampsia,' but then despite best efforts sometimes it was unpredictable and unavoidable.

'Not many believe in walking to a hospital during pregnancy until there is a problem.' The resident mused. 'Many first timers enter the hospital casualty with a baggage on their heads—a baggage called eclampsia.'

There was a separate room dedicated to these women, the 'eclampsia room'. As we walked into the labour room corridor, we saw at least four patients inside the eclampsia room. Two of them had delivered and two were in labour.

Out of these two, one was critical. She was nearly nine months pregnant; her husband found her at home a little disoriented, holding her head tightly in her hands. He took her to the district centre where they referred her immediately to the city hospital. It took him about four hours to arrange conveyance and reach here. She, meanwhile, went into labour and had a bout of convulsions on the way to the hospital. No sooner had she entered the labour room that she threw up another one. Her injured tongue and altered consciousness bore testimony to her altered physiology.

The idea was to deliver her fast. She was started on anticonvulsants and the labour augmented. The BP recording flashed 180/110.

'Did she ever have a high blood pressure in her pregnancy?'

'*Hamein kya pata* (How do we know)?' Her husband replied insolently.

'Are you carrying any papers with you?'

'Which papers, Madam*ji*?' Some people answered a question with a question.

'*Kabhi kisi doctor ko nahi dikhaya* (Have you never consulted a doctor)?'

'*Bimaar na padi toh hospital kyu jayein* (She was never ill, so why go to a hospital)?'

Another question! Was it guilt or plain ignorance? His repeated questions were jarring and getting more defiant.

He had to be informed about the high-risk situation. It was written down in Hindi and explained to him.

'Bimaar padi to tumhare paas liwa layen. Gaon walon ne to nahi kaha tha ki ye itni serious hai (She fell sick so I brought her here. The villagers never told me she was so serious).'

He signed the papers but still looked at them suspiciously.

'Garib hain, private mein nahi ja sakte. Par iska matlab ye nahi ki tum humko darao dhamkao (We are poor, can't afford to go to a private hospital, but that doesn't mean that you should scare me or threaten me).'

Caught in deep-rooted traditions and beliefs, he overlooked his omissions that could have prevented the catastrophe.

The next few hours saw her delivering but then she plunged into deep coma. She was fast losing touch with the mortal world and despite best efforts refused to be drawn out.

Her husband was understandably heartbroken, his grief unfathomable. But what followed later was beyond belief.

They had barely left with the body of the woman that the ward *bai* came rushing inside, scared to the core.

'Madam, he is coming back! And I think he is carrying a knife.' She said anxiously.

There was a collective gasp. These were the times when you were reminded of your vulnerability. The doors and windows offered no solace. These were also the times when you were reminded of the gaping security in a place we worked round the clock. The hospital took pride in its ancient heritage, which meant that there were hardly any proper bolts or locks. Most of the doors could not withstand even a friendly kick.

'Somebody inform the security and call the police.' Came a petrified voice from the labour room.

'Call the boys from the hostel.' The RSO, scared out of her wits, could hardly control her shaking voice.

'Madam, please go to the recovery room outside the operation theatre and lock it from inside.' The nurse said.

They ran off towards the recovery room which was the only room that boasted of some secure doors and windows.

The husband, mad with grief, lunged at them, flashing his knife dangerously. He had lost his mental balance and ran after the duty doctors, all women.

'I want my wife back!' He screamed hysterically. 'You all have killed her. You threw her in the corner, left her to die.'

Most patients and attendants hid in their wards. A few trouble-mongers followed him.

'Such neglect just because it is a government hospital?' They added more fuel to the fire. 'Open the door.' The demented man thundered from outside.

Sometimes, revelling in our profession, we forget our inherent deficiencies and lack of physical strength.

'Oh god! Is no one going to help us? What if he breaks the door?' The RSO said in panic. The door shook badly with the constant thumping.

The security and staff posted in other wards rushed towards the room. The man was overpowered, but not before the doctors inside had spent some gruelling moments, fearing for their lives.

'I will see you all. My wife's sacrifice will not go in vain.' His blood-shot eyes looked dangerous as he threatened even while he was forcefully dragged away.

It was difficult to draw the frightened doctors away from the room.

'We can't go to the labour room again.' They sobbed, still in shock.

The medical superintendent and the head of the department had arrived. The resident doctors were in no state to work and were sent home.

Every patient walking into a hospital hoped to survive. But every time a patient died, it could not be the fault of the doctors. However, there were very few willing to accept this.

The consultants were forced to look after the patients that night. If this was not bad enough, the coming days proved to be worse.

The lectures generally started from 8 am. Medicos were nocturnal people; early mornings were definitely not their favourite time especially for the hostellers. So, that explained them rushing to the classroom with milk pouches in their hands. Not everyone had the time or inclination to boil it. Surprisingly, the lecture hall wore a deserted look that day.

Varun sipped the milk nosily and grumbled.

'I would have slept a little more.' It was obvious he didn't believe in early morning baths either.

'Hey guys, did you hear that the Junior Doctors' Association (JDA) has gone on a strike?' Raj announced excitedly.

'Wow, so that means no classes!' The class replied in chorus.

'I just saw "his" scooter parked outside the hospital. Let's walk up to there,' shrieked Kavya. She was too gung-ho over the ENT guys these days.

Life had different priorities for everyone.

'*The Medical Students' Association* will decide whether they want to support the JDA in their strike. But yes, it definitely means no clinical classes for now,' it was announced.

That opened a plethora of possibilities. The day suddenly looked much brighter, carefree and happier.

From movies, to picnics, to just ogling at our seniors, there was no dearth of plans.

However, the ground situation was quite serious and was followed by a general body meeting and association discussions.

The incident of the previous day had spread like fire. It had laid bare the non-existent security for doctors and the callous attitude of some people towards the medical fraternity. It also showed how vulnerable our profession made us in the hands of disgruntled people.

Tension flared up between the doctors and the administration. There were a lot of protests. The resident doctors continued their strike, joined by the medical students. It was decided to take up many other pertinent issues with the administration. Issues like vanishing resources, poor infrastructure, absent power backup, meagre supply of gauze, gloves, syringes, and the essential commodities like medicines and sutures were all brought up.

'How can we go on risking our lives? We are the ones who are in the line of fire, facing public ire. The administration has made us their *bali ka bakra* (sacrificial lamb).' The JDA president roared. The hall echoed with claps of agreement.

The agony of the residents had spilled outside the hospital onto the roads leading to the office of the medical superintendent.

Those were the most memorable days, spent on the college ground indulging in silly, gibberish talk. Not many were keen to go home, even the hostellers preferred to stay back. This was no less than the college festivals. From lazy afternoons spent in the college lawns, to cosy dinners with friends, to the trips to the Tigda Dam, everyone had an alternative plan up their sleeves.

Meanwhile, the hospital was getting crippled and the patients were suffering. Eventually in the interest of the patients, a compromise was reached. The security was beefed up. There was now a police post just outside the labour room. Armed guards were also deployed. With the reassurance from the administration for their continuous support in raising the bars in providing quality healthcare, the junior doctors called off the strike and were back at the hospital.

There was a flurry of movement in the antenatal ward. A patient admitted in the ward had started having pains. Rather than calling the doctor on duty, the attendants preferred to walk her to the labour room. Walking was presumed to expedite labour and a successful delivery.

As she entered the labour room, her pains had visibly increased. She lay on the table groaning. This was her fifth pregnancy, but only one previous live birth.

Meanwhile, the labour room was once again caught in the middle of a storm. The shortage of staff could never be more acutely felt.

The patient was laid down on the table. As soon as she was uncovered, the diagnosis was clear.

The cord was hanging outside and along with it was a hand. Thankfully, it was moving.

The RSO looked around and shouted for help.

'Hey, come fast. This is transverse lie with hand and cord prolapse.' She had already pushed the cord inside again and was keeping the hand firmly inside as well.

'The cord pulsations are there. Ma'am, rush to the operation theatre and get things ready for caesarean.' She called out to her senior.

The senior rushed towards the operation theatre.

'Can you please come here?'

I was surprised to see her pointing towards me.

'Wear the gloves and come over. Keep your fingers where I tell you. The idea is to keep the pressure away from the cord. If it gets pressed the blood supply to the baby stops. Your fingers shall be inside even while she gets transferred and moves inside the theatre.' She explained.

To say that I was conscious would be underplaying it. I was positively nervous. Yet, I had no choice. The other doctors had to look after the labour room and there was no other help.

I kept my finger inside lifting the presenting part above the cord. I didn't think of anything beyond that and laboured just as much as the patient to keep my hands there. The patient was shifted on a trolley to the operation theatre. Neither of us was given an opportunity to change. Infection and sterility control was not a priority at this stage. It was a 'do-or-die' kind of situation.

Everyone shouted at me. 'Keep the hand there. Don't move.'

My hands were getting cramped up but an unknown force held me there. As I tried to twist my hands inside, suddenly I felt my fingers being grasped by something. I shouted, 'Someone is holding my hand!'

It took a second for all of us to realise that it was baby's hand that had prolapsed outside along with the cord that had gripped me.

'It means the baby is doing well. Great!' The other doctors exclaimed.

It was a strange feeling. Was the baby reassuring me or was it seeking solace?

'Don't worry, little one. We shall see you through.' I clasped the tiny hand in a silent promise.

The surgeon made a cut on the uterus and I felt the baby being pulled out from the above. I had to let the hand go.

The baby was born, a little distressed but soon her cry brought a visible sigh of relief on everyone's face.

I peered at her. Would she ever remember the hand that she had clung to even before she was born? I knew the answer. I was the one who would never forget this.

Where else could you be a part of this out-of-the-world, divine experience? Medicine had its lows but could any 'high' ever measure up to this?

Our gynae posting was coming to an end and so was our final professional. The studies heaped up to become the unattainable Mt Everest, the stress as deep as an ocean and the exams as unfathomable as an enemy bent upon a war.

If our theory exams tested our tenacity, the practicals were hell-bent on taking us back to being the most crude and primitive species alive, surviving on bare minimums. And the examiners tested the patience of even the toughest.

The *gudda* was in the breech position, with his body hanging outside and the head still stuck there.

'Spot diagnosis?' The examiner asked.

My batchmate Parul sat tense and haltingly answered, 'Arrest of the aftercoming head in breech presentation.'

'Good. So tell us, how would you proceed?'

'I will examine her.' Parul continued confidently. She placed an imaginary hand on the abdomen and in a blatant display of confidence went on to describe all the obstetric grips.

'The fundal grip?' The examiner asked.

'I shall feel the head of the baby.'

'Lateral grip?' The examiner smiled. The internal was staring at her, dropping hints but oblivious to all Parul continued.

'The lateral grips shall show the back on one side and limbs on another.' She was unstoppable as she went on to describe in lucid details.

The examiner was fast losing patience. 'But the baby is lying outside,' she snapped.

There was a round of laughter. Parul realised her mistake and flushed red.

The examiner shook her head and pointed towards the instruments. But Parul's confidence was broken and never recovered.

The next student was more confident but then when it came to drugs, he just couldn't differentiate between prostaglandins and progesterones. It was funny as he went on elaborating one under the name of another and obviously it was a disaster.

The examiners were grown-up people, tolerant and understood the turmoil that built up before the final professional exams. They had learned to look beyond the minor failings too.

Like the one who was given the dummy pelvis with the foetus in breech presentation. He refused to deliver the baby vaginally but insisted on doing a version, turning the baby and bringing the head down. The examiners tried to dissuade him but he persisted. Well, it was again a losing art and they couldn't help but encourage him finally. The examiners too were entitled to their moments of reprieve! The four-day-long practical exams were testing their patience too.

I was now getting really nervous. This was a specimen of the uterus till the other day that I had seen in our lab. The only difference being that they had sliced it and it showed like a cut surface. The examiner was now insisting that it was not an uterus!

'Kidney?' I had said it aloud and saw the examiner smiling. I breathed a smile of relief.

'But, why kidney?' The examiner asked.

There went all my preparations of the day before. Yet my love for the surgery textbook, *Bailey and Love* saved my day.

'A gynaecologist would think twice before venturing into that area.' The examiner leaned back and said.

'Tell me, Lady, what are the three most common mistakes you make while doing hysterectomy?' The examiner posed the next question.

I shifted uncomfortably. I didn't mind being called a lady, but not like this. This spoke of an impending disaster. I could sense that.

I enumerated all the possible complications that I had read about but the examiner was nowhere impressed.

I was about to give up when the examiner smiled, 'Okay young lady, I will tell you the first one.'

I bristled at the 'lady' but kept quiet. She had my attention now.

'You cut the right ureter!'

Okay, I had heard about the surgeons ridiculing the gynaecologists on that.

'We rescue them,' they would say smugly.

I never quite liked the sarcasm. 'The gynae consultant will cut the ureter, or injure the bladder and then they set the house in turmoil. Our house surgeon will come and stitch it calmly.' The surgeons would boast.

It was an exaggeration.

'So, tell me the other two reasons.' The examiner prodded.

I struggled but failed to come up with a satisfactory answer. The examiner was feeling probably kind and decided to bail me out.

'I think we have given you enough time. So, let me tell you now. The gynaecologist first cuts the right ureter.' She looked around and continued, 'She then cuts the left ureter.'

What kind of sadism was my examiner suffering from to indulge in this self-mockery? I could sense my internals were not pleased about this as well.

'So now can you guess the third?'

I shook my head.

'She cuts both the ureters.' The external examiner burst out laughing. 'Come on people, it's just a joke.'

I listened quietly as others joined her reluctantly, not knowing exactly what to do.

I lamented the stereotypes which the most sincere and laborious department suffered from.

As always, I was in the last batch of practicals and with us the curtains were drawn on the toughest of exams—the final professional or the final-year MBBS exams.

'How was your exam today?' My mother asked.

'They are over.' Exams were no longer good or bad.

It was the same answer that she had been hearing for the last five years. She sighed with relief.

She could finally watch the cricket match on TV today with the volume on.

And soon, we would start a new journey, of practical training, our internship—the 'honeymoon' period of medicine where we would be paid a stipend! A precious Rs 1,340! This was archaic, almost a British legacy that the management refused to change, yet it did nothing to dampen our spirit.

Internship

'I am a surgeon with a scalpel for false values.'

—Lenny Bruce

It was a strange feeling to cut through the layers of the patient's perineum. There! My first surgical incision! If I felt scared I didn't show it, neither did it reflect in my hand that cut boldly. Well, not quite! I just stopped short and ended up giving a small episiotomy. I had seen them doing it so many times and had mentally revised it many other times.

I had waited anxiously. The foetal head teased me but never stayed there enough to bestow upon me the moment of 'crowning' glory.

'Rama *bai,* please come now. You will have to help the patient.' The ward *bai* took position.

Help meant she would give some pressure from the top of the patient's abdomen. You didn't have to mention it but many patients owed their normal deliveries to this fundal pressure.

With every pain the patient brought her chin forward and pushed.

'*Push kar push kar, zor lag zor laga.*' This never failed to amuse us especially now that Pushkar had joined the paediatric department as a postgraduate. He was constantly teased for his name being chanted by the labour room girls.

Meanwhile, with every pain the ward *bai* pushed the head from above.

'Suno, todna nahi is baar.' She meant not to break the pain.

Suddenly, the patient gripped her thighs, pursed her lips and groaned. This was a good pain and there it was—'crowned' and almost waiting for me to give that incision. No sooner had I given the episiotomy, that the baby delivered.

'Well done.' My senior said appreciatively.

May be this one would have come out without an episiotomy. I flushed guiltily. At least it had delivered easily. I tried to justify myself.

Skin, subcutaneous tissue, muscle and then the mucosa, the layers lay exposed to my dissecting eyes. However, the field got soiled by bleeding.

'Pressure, packing and suture.' The three basic principles in controlling the bleeding!

Now lay the next step, stitching the episiotomy. Into my internship I had assisted my seniors in this process many times. I knew how to place the knots but I had never repaired it without supervision.

I looked around. It was well past midnight and my senior was nowhere to be seen. Did she trust my surgical abilities more than I did myself? I wondered humorously and stared at my operating field soiled with blood. I needed to stitch it fast.

But a stitch needed a suture material. Neither the hospital nor the patients could afford brand new ones. It was always in short supply. The leftovers from the previous ones were never discarded. We were very economical and didn't believe in wasting our scarce resources.

I looked inside the boiler. It was empty. I was now worried.

There was no one around. The stage was set and I was in charge of the show, by default.

'Sister, do you have chromic catgut?' The nurse shook her head. I called up the Kamla Raja Hospital's operation theatre.

'No, who is this?' A rude voice from the other end replied.

I kept the phone down. I called up the JA Hospital's operation theatre.

'We don't have any. Why don't you check with your own labour room in-charge?' I was told.

I was now getting desperate. I looked helplessly at the nurse but she looked away.

Could I ask the attendants? What if they complained?

I slowly tiptoed into the doctors' duty room. The tired doctors were sleeping. They had been working non-stop for more than 24 hours. The pre-PG entrance exams also had been stalled resulting in acute crunch of house surgeons. As a result, the interns got lots of hands-on experience. The bad part was that certain departments hardly left us with any time for studying. The obstetrics and gynaecology department was one such department. With its huge work load and a pile of paper work, manpower was always in shortage. These days it had become pathetic.

I felt through the pockets of their aprons guiltily. Nothing there. Now what? I walked out silently not wanting to disturb them.

Back in the labour room I looked at the nurse again. She sighed and went to look into the boiler.

'There is a small one.' She said pointing inside.

I rushed. Almost hidden in the cervices of the boiler, lay a small piece. I looked at it doubtfully.

It was small but the incision was also not very big.

'You can try.' The nurse looked at me encouragingly.

Try I did! At first, a little awkwardly, then tentatively, and finally boldly.

Something inside me took over. The baby steps of a surgeon! My hands were writing my destiny.

There was a strange thrill. Like putting in order every layer, step-by-step. I fumbled again while taking the knots. The early ones were a little tricky, the later ones a little short of being perfect.

'Take a thread and practice at home.' That's what I had been told.

'The best knots aren't the one practiced on a human body but at your dining table.'

That's precisely where I had been practicing. I was now using all the skills I had acquired over the last few days.

In the end, order was regained at the body planes and tissue approximated nicely in a beautiful stitch line. This was a definite high, one like I had never had before.

'A scar is a surgeon's autograph.' I remembered the old saying.

Pleased with my handiwork I gazed at it with wonder.

Just as I got back to writing the notes my senior entered, tired and yawning. Her 'sleep time' was over. The nurse told her about our 'lost and found' suture and my surgical feat.

'Oh, you should have asked me.' She slowly pulled out a brand new suture from her bag.

I was zapped. All my efforts went in vain! The 'suture' silently mocked me. Was I being unnecessarily responsible?

The responsibility of an intern was as much fictitious as the ghosts who inhabited the wards. Never seen and promptly forgotten once they got on with their preparations for the mighty pre-PG entrance exams.

However, I had relished my first independent suturing. Whenever I closed my eyes I could see my fingers working deftly, suturing opposing tissue together and tying the knots.

'You have nothing else to dream about.' Kavya teased me. She was drooling over the orthopaedic resident these days. Her fascination for the ENT guy was now a thing of the past.

The seed for my future had been sown. Everyday, my fascination for surgery was growing.

During my MBBS days and even later as an intern I loved surgery. The textbook *Bailey and Love* was like my Bhagwad Gita. But general surgery was definitely not my cup of tea. I disliked doing the hydroceles, hernias and the extensive dressings of large-infected wounds. I would gladly stay away from it any given day. Despite the clinical neutrality of a doctor, male patients made me uncomfortable.

The memories of the last time that I had seen a male patient still coloured me red.

'Oh my god, it is moving!' I squirmed.

An anatomical fact stood proud in its physiology. I stared at it in shocked disbelief. The damn thing had moved further.

Soon it was going to be my turn to go near it. I looked around. Every face wore the picture of clinical impassiveness, not giving anything away. I turned astonished eyes towards the other girls. Swati had come back. Her head was low and she took back her place. The boys stood at the other side quietly. As it is we were not supposed to speak in Dr Sharma's clinics. He did all the talking and didn't like any voice of diffidence. But, he taught well so we tolerated his arrogance.

Today, he was demonstrating the inguinal lymph nodes. A young, rural male was the 'case', the exhibit. The poor man had turned his face to one side while his anatomy lay helpless under Dr Sharma's physiology class. Ruthlessly dissected by the curious medicos, our 'case' could barely disguise his torment.

It was my turn and the damn thing was at its peak. I was rooted to the spot. All eyes appeared to be silently challenging me. Would I look gauche if I refused? No! Doctors were supposed to be beyond these things.

Though I had been in the department for more than two months, I had barely managed beyond hernias and hydroceles.

'There is a proper way to hold the hydrocele.' I revulsed yet I had held it between the index and middle finger of both my hands just as Dr Sharma demonstrated.

The continuous display of the male anatomy was killing my passion for surgery. My reverie broken, I felt my arm suddenly clamped from behind and my friend, Swati whispered in my ears. 'Look at the poor guy. Why do you want to embarrass him?' I reddened. If only she knew what I was going through. I felt the compelling eyes of Dr Sharma and brushing off her hand I moved.

Inspection and then palpation, the rules of surgical examination mocked me. We were doctors, not schoolgirls.

The 'case' had covered his eyes, turned away from his erection. My hands shot forward and quickly touched the small nodular swellings, lying in a chain in his groin. I wondered what infection would have enlarged them. It took away my mind from the glaring truth I was trying to ignore.

Hurriedly I came back to my place before another girl went forward. Phew! That was close. I would have to take some other branch after MBBS. My love for *Bailey and Love* had to be sacrificed. The department of surgery was definitely out of bounds for me.

Soon, it was the turn of the boys but by that time probably the torment of the 'case' had got through Dr Sharma. He asked him to get up and go back to his bed. I wondered how many poor people would make the supreme sacrifice to teach us.

'Did you know Dr Sharma was scolding the "case"?' Kavya remarked.

I shook my head.

'I was standing next to him. The moment the damn thing started moving he got agitated and said to the patient, "Stop it, I said just stop it. I had told you there would be girls here." But the poor guy was beyond control.' We laughed. The guys too joined in.

'Do you know about the last case of hernia that Dr Sharma showed us?' Sameer asked.

We didn't.

'You girls didn't come for that class and well, it wasn't Dr Sharma who missed you the most. It was that patient.'

Our eyes rolled up in disbelief.

'He was categorical that he had agreed to be examined on the condition that there would be girls there. But all he got were male students.'

Some 'disappointments' were so funny.

Obstetrics and gynaecology was a branch where I had a sense of belonging. I was quite comfortable seeing female rather than male patients and, the joy of life giving its first cry enthralled me. I knew this was where I was meant to be. This was again a branch that unlike others hardly needed any super specialisation. I would finally break the shackles of books. The last few years had barely been without a book or bereft of an exam.

In my naivety, I was opting for a life that would demand more and stretch all the boundaries. But then this was not the time to ponder. One had to cross the limit to discover the limitless. I was gearing up for a journey, labouring to open my eyes to a unique world, a world of obstetrics and gynaecology!

And this time I was here to stay.

Post-graduation

'We have turned doctors into gods and worship their deity by offering up our bodies and our souls, not to mention our worldly goods.

And yet paradoxically, they are the most vulnerable of human beings. Their suicide rate is eight times the national average. Their percentage of drug addiction is one hundred times higher.

And because they are painfully aware that they cannot live up to our expectations, their anguish is unquantifiably intense. They have been aptly called the "wounded healers"...'

—*Doctors*, Erich Segal

The first time you feel like a doctor is when you get through your premedical entrance test. Even your neighbours profess admiration. But it all gets drowned on the very first day at the college and before you know you are swept by the tide called medical studies. Soon, the final year dawns making you the senior most in the college. Then one day you pass your final professional exams and finally, get to add that much precious prefix 'doctor' to your name. This time around, your neighbours look at you with awe and respect. Now you understand majority of their ailments even though you can't treat them. But you can guide them around the hospital. They shall forever value your acquaintance.

Internship teaches you what your textbooks could never do. It is a chance to get real as a doctor. But, as the shadow of the pre-PG entrance exams looms large, interns soon become a disappearing specie in the hospital.

Once through the hardship of the mighty pre-PG exams, you get a branch of your choice. You think that you have finally made it when you realise that people your age are getting married and some even having kids. And here you are…one-third of your life gone! Those who intern in government hospitals still earn a stipend but those interning in private hospitals end up paying themselves. Meanwhile, your other friends are buying a car or even a house!

'So when are you going to earn?'

The prospect of forever supporting their progeny starts worrying the parents.

'Don't worry, Mummy, once I finish my post-graduation I would get a job.' I was keeping my fingers crossed.

Jobs were few in the government hospitals and the corporates wanted those with special skills or a practice.

An MBBS without a PG is a struggle in a world that now recognises only specialists. A post-graduation would take three more years but probably life would then move on a stable track. Some of us would move to practice after this, some would continue with senior residency and sharpen their skills. The more ambitious ones would aspire for super specialisation.

At least we were now senior enough to command our way in the hospital. Or was it?

On the very first day itself as a postgraduate, you realise you are back at square one. You are the junior most but unlike before, you are neither indulged in nor handled with kid gloves. Your well-being is lowest in the list of priorities in a teaching hospital. You work the most yet your work is the least recognised; you labour for your ward but your senior gets all the accolades but if anything goes wrong, all the fingers point at you. After all you are the first-year PG—the house surgeon.

'Today, I welcome all the house surgeons. I leave the house to you.' The head of department greeted us.

I looked at Kavya. I was glad to have my friend along with me in this journey.

'You are married to this house. You shall now be the shadows that will guard it. You may not be seen. The world may be blind to you. But your house shall show your presence to everyone. A clean, well-organised, smoothly running house. That will be your greatest presence.'

A marriage. Seriously!

'We are gaining too many mothers-in-law.' Parul whispered looking at a sea of seniors.

Kavya, Parul, Swati and Payal from my own college had made it to my department. There were two more girls, Bani and Rashmi from another college and much to our consternation, a male doctor, Dr Anuj, joined our all-girls' squad. I looked at him doubtfully.

'Would he relate to a woman's problem and would patients be comfortable with him?' I asked. Kavya shrugged.

Most of those who made it to this department as PGs were toppers yet they were often made the butt of jokes and generally projected as hyper, flustered or confused girls.

'They shout at the drop of hat and somehow don't have their basics right.' The physician sneered.

'At the first hint of complication they will call a surgeon, any medical problems they will refer to a physician.' The all-knowing '*Narad Munis*' of the hospital, the anaesthetists added their valuable input brazenly. Passing smart comments was their birthright and they never missed a chance to exercise it.

'The cerebral value is err…less and the girls work on a spinal level,' jeered the surgeons. This was rich coming from those who were perennially in doubt, never thinking beyond following the dictum 'when in doubt, open and see'.

'Do you know the "torch test" for gynaecologist?' The paediatrician asked seriously.

I had never heard of this one!

'When you put the torch on one side of the head and the light comes out from the other side, you know it's the gynaecologist's head!' He explained to me.

This was height of insolence! I squirmed even while the rest of them rolled in laughter.

Barring gynaecology and obstetrics, every other department was presumably about brains. We were pretty much projected as midwives. This was the worst slur. Probably it was about being a 'women's department' and therefore suffered from a gender insensitivity. Reality was so very different.

Some of the doctors got married during their post-graduation, some got pregnant too. Sometimes they had to cook, sometimes their babies fell sick and then some of them went on maternity leaves. As women, compulsions in life caught up with them along with their studies. Not that they got much leaves or special privileges during their pregnancies. Ironically, the very department that taught everyone to rest during pregnancy, was at times apathetic about their own pregnant doctors.

The understaffed departments didn't have much choice either. The work burden had to be shared by the other residents. The residents would end up cribbing about the newly married or the pregnant ones. And of course working the way they did, the stress at work soon started influencing their pregnancies so that their pregnancies were generally 'high risk'.

The routine hours started generally at 8 am and majority reached home at around 5 pm. The ones on emergency duty stayed back longer.

There were no weekly offs. Though, officially Sunday was 9 to 11 am, for the consultants it was a holiday and they turned up late for the rounds. So, the residents generally got free by 2 pm or later. The only reprieve being that on Sundays there were only rounds, no routine surgeries or blood investigations to be sent.

The Kamla Raja Hospital, meant for only women and children was literally going to be our residence, and true to its meaning, the residency days would hardly leave time for anywhere or anything else.

It was the first day of my emergency duty.

After slogging in the wards since morning with a pile of case sheets and a very unfriendly nurse, it was not something I was looking forward to. The reporting time to the labour room was at 2 pm. Here, the residents from different wards gave 'over' of the important patients in their wards.

Strangely the same seniors who had been so loving all those years in the medical school suddenly were draconian.

My first posting was in the post-operative ward. Here the nursing in-charge, Sister Bhalla was somebody everyone was wary of.

'She is quite close to the professor. It is important to be in her good books,' my seniors had warned.

There was not much you could demand from the nurses. From starting IV lines, taking out blood samples, removing catheters to dressings and even during rounds, they were conspicuously absent. It was only when the consultants came on rounds that they made a friendly appearance.

They had a strange penchant nonetheless—snooping on the resident doctors and reporting them to the professor. If you had friends especially those of the opposite sex dropping in your ward for even a casual hello, it would be noticed. The professor was conservative and such things didn't go down very well with her.

While we sat with a small table and chair in the wards, Sister Bhalla had a room to herself and that room was adorned with a well-equipped almirah.

Just like our kit, she too kept her emergency stuff ready and strictly used them in case of an 'emergency'.

Sometimes it opened for the VIP patients as well. A VIP patient was not one by designation, but usually the private patients of the boss. Rarely, she extended the privilege to the residents too but that needed the highest degree of motivation. She needed to be exceptionally impressed for that.

Sister Bhalla was an astute women and she never missed anything. She quietly noted when you chatted with other teachers, especially Dr Bali. She dutifully put it across to the professor, who didn't get along well with Dr Bali at all.

The harassed eyes of the 'resident' could not see beyond these manipulations. They even failed to appreciate the hard work of the nurses that went into keeping the wards clean, the struggle to provide the basic antibiotics and other medicines daily in a paucity-driven hospital, the toil it took for the nurses in dealing with the lower staff.

Out of the safe cocoons of our MBBS days we were out in the open, on our own facing the rude real world where rivalry, jealousy and insecurities raised their ugly heads in every nook and corner.

We were the house surgeons, the anonymous face in a ' house of doctors', straight in the line of fire from a 'house of patients'.

It was almost three in the afternoon. Every single bone hurt in our body. Kavya and I stretched our tired limbs. We were working nonstop from 8 am. The labour room that was passed on to us was a mess. From making case sheets, to putting down notes and getting patients moved, we realised we were now both the administrators and the clinicians.

'Your documentation should never be lagging. This is the evidence of your presence. Verbal assurances have no standing. If you have seen and not noted it down it means you have not seen the patient.'

There was no dearth of high-risk patients. And that meant charting of vitals at least every two hours.

We had been instructed to bring our own blood pressure instruments. It was mandatory. Carrying it along we jetted from the 'eclampsia room' to the septic labour room to back in the labour room, busy putting notes in case sheets which hardly had any paper left. Paper was again a precious commodity.

All patients in labour needed to have the foetal heart rate checked every 30 minutes in the first stage and every five minutes in the second stage of labour. The goals were predictably not always reached. But even the struggle to achieve them was a strain.

While the labour room clamoured for calm, our hungry stomachs cried for food. Lunch break was for one hour. Kavya's home was near but mine was out of question.

'It is almost an hour. Let's go back.' Kavya's tired voice broke through. Now lethargic after food, our bodies were reluctant to move.

'Let's sleep for a while. I am sure one hour can't mean just 60 minutes. We don't have to rush back soon.' I said.

She readily gave in and we closed our eyes. Half an hour later we were being woken up by Aunty with a cup of tea. We quickly had our tea and rushed back.

'Is this the time to come back? You juniors have no respect for time these days.' An angry voice welcomed us back.

'We are just two people here. There are two caesareans to be shifted, and many more lined up. So much work is pending. Who do you think will do all that?' Dr Neera, our senior went on.

Sometimes it was better to keep quiet.

'Kavya, you go to the operation theatre and you, stay here.' Dr Neera said, pointing towards me. 'Call us if there is any problem.' With that she left the labour room.

'Poor girl, didn't even have anything to eat. There was such a huge tide of patients.' The nurse told us disapprovingly.

If that was supposed to make me feel guilty, it did!

It also set the tempo for the coming emergency duties.

After midnight, provided there was nothing active going on, the seniors went to take rest. The house surgeon took turns in taking a break to stretch their tired bodies. But this was not a rule. A 'rush' would break this and bring them all back to the labour room at a war footing.

Our biological clock was rebooted, factory settings changed, reset to work mechanically. By the time we reached home after working more than 36 hours at a stretch, we could just flop on the bed and sleep!

Kavya and I were happy becoming a team. We had been close friends for long and enjoyed a good rapport with most of our seniors who were known to us from our MBBS days.

But soon many of our seniors objected to our pairing up for emergency duties.

'It's not fair. How could Neera take both of them under herself?' The final year PGs cribbed.

Neera was the senior RSO in charge of the duty roster.

'I have a gut feeling that it's not a mere coincidence we are posted with her on most emergencies.' Kavya confided in me.

She was right and this was not going down well with her batchmates.

'Neera is so manipulative! Why should she keep all the good workers with her?' Came another rant from a senior.

'We are in demand, Kavya.' It felt good to be the 'bone of contention' between the seniors.

Ours was a story too good to be true. Predictably, very soon we headed for a split. Our seniors made sure that we were paired with different house surgeons.

'The good house surgeons should work separately, just to keep work going smoothly.'

'Don't feel bereft.' I consoled Kavya. 'We are still in the same department.'

It was true. Though I still missed her comforting presence around me, it was only the emergencies which we were not doing together. While most of our friends were now in different departments, some even in different cities, we were fortunate to be at least together. The quest for specialisation had taken each one of us on different paths. Still, we were connected in our thoughts and in our minds, through common friends and through phone calls!

The house was gradually settling down with the new house surgeons and their kits. Our friends from other departments never failed to mock us, often catching us in the middle of the hospital corridors, looking obliquely at our kits.

'Ah, your travel bags! Where are you off to?'

'You girls are rich!' They would sneer at us. We waited for everyone barring the emergency staff to go home, leaving the hospital to us. This was a high. That heady feeling of running the whole hospital by yourself!

And despite the workload the most carefree workers were still the house surgeons. Away from the exams, they were least bothered by the hierarchy or the paraphernalia that bogged the senior PGs. Books had not even been bought. The seniors shielded them, faced the music, even if the house surgeons were the ones who messed it.

The duty of looking after the house also meant keeping the duty rooms tidy. It was our job to see that the water coolers were working and their tank of water full.

The only people we could casually command were our interns.

House job was also a period when we carried the hierarchy home. The few hours at home passed out in sleep or in a trance. We were hardly productive to our families anymore.

The initial days were difficult and sometimes they got ridiculous too.

Back home after one such long duty I was sleeping when suddenly I felt the water cooler start throwing warm air.

My sleep-deprived mind could hardly comprehend much.

'The water is finished.' I could hear my mother saying.

'We need to refill it.' She was speaking to my brother.

'Ask the intern to come and fill it.' I spoke authoritatively.

'What?' My mother just couldn't understand what was going on.

'The intern, Mummy!' I repeated with irritation.

It was some time later, with bouts of laughter jarring my senses that I woke up.

This incidence showed how deep-rooted our house job was delving into our lives, leaving a mark on our families as well.

House job was also the time to build lasting relationships with other staff.

We had already learned not to cross our paths with the nurses in-charge, we therefore, reached out to the junior nurses. The ward nurses and the junior staff were nice and cooperative. This also extended to helping each other in our moments of distress.

Many of the nurses were competent enough to conduct deliveries and even stitch the episiotomies back. Most of the house surgeons, left alone with them in the labour room, had learned the techniques of delivery from the nurses. Whenever we got restless, they taught us patience while encouraging patients to bear down. In the difficult cases when both the patient and even the doctor gave up, they took charge. From motivating the patients to giving that fundal pressure from above, they were our partners at every step and we learned to live in peaceful coexistence.

'*Rani,* sit on your bed and bear down!' The patient would look hopefully at the nurse. 'I will help you from above.' She would take a strategic position by her side.

They had their own beliefs, their own ways and generally we didn't cross each other.

'Hold this strand of hair in between your lips, *Rani*.' We shook our head.

'No, Madam, don't laugh. This will make the placenta separate.'

We could just smile at them indulgently. But they were very confident about these things they called '*totke*'. Even the patients trusted them, sometimes more than us.

'Madam, *thodi der aur try kar lo. Fir caesarean kar dena* (Try a little longer, then do caesarean).' A silent look would pass between the attendants and the midwife. Unaware to us, an understanding had been reached outside. The caesarean was withheld and the trial of labour went on.

Not all trials were failures. Sometimes miracles happened. After all this is what life was all about, it was never simple mathematics. And it defied all logic, even the ones taught in the text book.

It did make us sheepish initially but then with maturity came acceptance. There was no place for ego. It was the 'delivery' that counted; a live, healthy one. That was the only saving grace. Rest everything was forgotten or ignored.

Emergency was heralded by accepting the 'hand over' sheet, sticking it up on the clip boards and then accepting the welcome tea from the staff.

The hospitals also made you empathetic towards the other staff that worked here. While the residents were still under training and were getting a stipend, majority of the staff were here to earn. They worked to feed their hungry stomachs, struggled to make their ends meet.

So, it went without saying that the ward *bais* didn't take it kindly when disturbed during their 'meal time'.

'Shanti*bai,* please shift bed no. 4 to the post-natal ward.'

There were more labouring patients than the available labour tables. Shifting the delivered ones fast brought in more available beds.

There was hardly anything left that was not the duty of the house surgeon. Shifting of the patient was thankfully not one of them. We had to depend on these ward *bais*.

But they had more pressing needs.

'Madam, *khane ke liye to kaam karte hain. Shanti se do roti bhi nahi khane deti ho tum* (Madam, we work hard to earn food, but you do not even let us eat a square meal in peace).' The ward *bai* complained.

There was no point getting worked up. Unless a dire emergency we did not encroach upon their private moment. Not that they minded shifting the delivered patients. Most of them looked forward to it. This was their moment of extra earnings.

Most families gave away generously when they had a baby, especially a baby boy. It was considered a good omen. The ward *bais* took it as their birthright and some of them learned to hold that as ransom to shifting the patients and the babies. The glaring gender discrimination, evident right from the cradle!

The news of a baby girl born was met with as much dejection with the ward *bais* as the baby's family. A source of income was lost. They never asked for money. It was left on the generosity of the family members if they really wanted to give away.

This all flourished discreetly away from the eyes of the doctor. It took a few patients' complaints to know the gigantic proportion it had reached.

'They refused to shift the baby to the mother unless we paid.' A patient's husband complained.

'You should have complained,' I said.

'We were told that it would be futile as even the doctors had their share in this.' He said adding to our outrage.

'The ward *bai* took money to hand over even our still born.' Another aggrieved patient cried.

The ward *bai* was suspended but the damage to the reputation of the noble profession was done.

The workers had a strong union and it was at times difficult to take action against the erring staff. The hospital could never dream of working without the class-4 employees. And majority of them especially the ones who held permanent jobs were much aware of this.

There were a few places in the hospital which were spooky. This included the burns ward, the eclampsia room and the septic-labour room. They were shrouded with haunted tales. The senior staff and nurses particularly relished narrating them. Maybe they knew that it got under our skin.

There was undoubtedly a strange fascination about ghost stories.

'Madam, can you see the quadrangle?' One of the nurses asked me.

I stared outside the window of the labour room into the dark night.

'Kamla Raja used to walk down the central quadrangle in her famous white saree,' she said. Almost all the buildings in the city carried the legacy of the royal family of Gwalior.

I closed the window.

'You are just trying to scare me.' I had no inclination to know about her midnight rendezvous.

'No, Madam. Ask Bimla Sister. She will tell you about the anguished cries coming from the burns ward,' the nurse said.

I would remember not to walk that stretch in the night.

'I don't believe you.' I told her, although not very convincingly.

'I have heard the doors of the septic-labour room creaking in the middle of the night.' She said, adding, 'Madam, Bimla sister was on duty. She was asked to bring the dressing tray from the septic-labour room. As she reached there, she could hear footsteps following her.

She ignored it and went inside the room. A shadow crossed her and the moment she was inside the room, the door closed.'

'It must have been the wind.' I countered.

'No, Madam, there were no latches still she couldn't open the door. She screamed and when other people rushed inside she was lying on the floor, unconscious.'

'She must have been scared.' I reasoned.

'You don't believe us. She saw a woman lying on the bed, struggling as if she was in labour. The woman was all yellow. And then there was the sound of a baby crying. She could see no more and fainted.' The nurse said.

This was spine-chilling but I dared not admit it to her.

'A woman with jaundice had died there after giving birth to a dead baby. There are haunted corners around, Madam.'

I didn't want to hear anymore.

Most of these stories were fabricated, by-products of a fertile imagination. But try as I might, I couldn't shrug off these nocturnal visitors from my mind. Whenever I walked the silent corridors of the hospital at night, I would subconsciously look for them.

It didn't help if the night was rainy and stormy. The sound of thunder and lightning would not subdue the groaning of patients. It added to their woes.

And it didn't help either when there was a call from the surgical department.

'There's a woman with 90 percent burns. We have to go and see her.' My senior RSO, Dr Namita read out the call paper.

I recoiled. The memory from my surgical posting days during internship was still fresh.

'What are we going to do there?' I cribbed.

'She is three months pregnant.'

'Ouch! Do you think this could be bride burning? Dowry harassment?' I asked.

'I hope not. It shouldn't be a medico-legal case.' Dr Namita said.

The burn ward was at the far corner. One had to walk a lonely stretch to reach here.

'The souls of those who die a painful death are never free.' The voice of our labour-room nurse echoed with that of the thunder. I shuddered and looked around. The shadows were dancing crazily on the walls.

The patient was kept in a secluded cabin. A pair of eyes stared at us through her bandaged face.

'What happened?' I asked gently.

Her lips moved but she could barely speak and turned away restless. She must have been in lot of pain. Her whole body was covered with bandages. A woman who introduced herself as her mother replied instead.

'She was cooking and the stove turned over her. That's what we have been told.'

'She is pregnant, too?'

'Barely two months! She got married just three months back.'

I stopped myself from asking if she suspected her husband and in-laws. It was not within my purview.

She was groaning and it was difficult but we finished her examination and left her room.

Outside we were met by a man who interrupted us.

'Is she fine? Do you think she will make it?' He asked.

'You need to ask the surgeons for that. We have come from the obstetrics and gynaecology department.'

'Okay. But is the baby alright?'

'We will check that on ultrasound.'

'Thanks.' He smiled, but somehow it didn't quite reach his eyes.

By now we had seen many patients and their attendants. He didn't look like a grieving attendant.

'Sister, please keep the case sheets with you.' The case sheets needed to be handled carefully for sensitive patients.

'I think he is going to be arrested soon. They burned the poor woman.' The nurse said.

'Then why doesn't she say that?' I asked.

'I am sure she will. Right now she's scared. I have seen enough of them in the last few years in the burn ward to know. I have seen her expression every time he enters the room. Trust me, he and his family are guilty.'

It was not our job to speculate. We just prayed for the women lying inside and her unborn baby. The night was dark and the clouds thundered above. We rushed back to our labour room. Hopefully the sky would clear by morning.

Monsoons not only lead to mushrooming of just mosquitoes, insects and every other thing you wished was not ever born but also led to a downpour of deliveries in the labour room. And along with a spurt of deliveries came all kinds of infections. Almost every ward in the hospital would get full.

The night was pelting heavy rains and thunder as I sat down in the labour room.

Just as the rain started pattering on the window panes, the electricity went off. It was not something that happened infrequently but it was generally short lived.

'Sister, can you find out what's going on?'

The torch, a mandatory part of the kit, was the first thing to come out.

The nurse started making frantic calls.

'The transformer has tripped. They are trying to restore the line, but it will take some time.' She came back worriedly.

A patient let out a loud cry. All of us rushed to her side.

'Sister, please hold the torch.' The battery would also not last forever. Our nurses were smart enough to have an alternative in their cupboard. Soon candles were burning in the labour room offering some light.

It wasn't easy. As I strained in the dark labour room alone, I thought about the other team members in the operation theatre. I shuddered to imagine their fate.

While I sat down stitching the episiotomy of one patient in the candle light, the nurse cried out.

'Madam, this one is also delivering.'

I got up and rushed to the side of the other one. I really thanked my stars that I had at least a competent nurse with me.

One after the other, and sometimes simultaneously the patients were delivering.

'Sister, give me a pack.' I learned the skills of management here. While I packed one patient, I finished delivering the other and then went back to stitching them.

The skies were unrelenting and so was the defunct power supply. It was as if every force had turned against us.

Still we fought valiantly. The candles were kept for the labour room and deliveries. The torch was kept for the tricky situations that warranted more focussed light like stitching the episiotomy. Necessity as they say is the mother of invention. That day somehow between the doctors, nurses and our ward *bais* we had managed to deliver 15 patients and even shifted some of them to the post-natal wards.

The patients too were accommodating. Coming from less privileged circumstances, they adjusted to the situation better than us. Many of the attendants had brought their own candles. Some even kindly offered few for the labour room. It was coming together in difficult situations like these that one realised the value of tolerance and solidarity.

The morning rays were now filtering through the window lifting the darkness. The corridors wore testimony to the storm that had ravaged the night. Garbage, dust and leaves lay strewn across the corridors. The sweepers had started their morning round.

It was almost 8 am when there was a commotion outside. A patient had been brought from a nearby village.

Much to my dismay she turned out to be full-term pregnancy with bleeding. A placenta previa! That meant lots of consents, arranging blood and preparing for a caesarean section. Sighing, I went inside asking the patient to be brought in. If only the labour room rested or took a break!

As I waited, the patient didn't follow. I was exhausted. My duty would soon be over but it was unbecoming of a good resident to leave work unfinished. I needed to work her up.

'I am going to take the history outside.' I told the nurse and moved out of the labour room and literally bumped into our head of department.

'What are you doing? Patients are waiting outside and you are just roaming around?' She asked.

I fumbled. The papers in my hand were shadowed just like my toil all through the night.

I stared at her.

'This is the problem with the new generation. You just don't know how to organise your work. Sister, please shift the patient inside.'

The nurse who just had got the time to have her morning tea rushed outside. The poor thing was equally flustered.

'Can we now start the round of the labour room?' She ordered.

She must have known about our nightlong turmoil and how we held fort through the adversities. Yet one look at a patient waiting outside, one that had just arrived and she took it all wrong. Not a single word of appreciation. Was it too much to expect compassion from your professor? Did it go with their post to pass a sweeping judgment?

I fumed inwardly though I didn't utter a single word.

By the time we were halfway through the labour room, the team from the operation theatre had arrived. They had been gone for more than four hours.

'Operation finished? I hope everything went well.' She asked the senior RSO.

'Ma'am, it was tough. We literally worked in torch light.'

If it was a torture in the labour room it must have been hell for them during surgery. I could still bring the candle close but how can you have a burning candle inside an open abdomen.

Our boss simply nodded her head. Well, at least they got recognition. I smiled ruefully.

Sometimes in our zeal to set a good example we ended up as a horrible warning.

However, nothing could take away the sense of accomplishment I felt. The tenacity of a resident was here to stay, despite all odds.

The two-hour respite that we got post duty sometimes gave a whole lot of sense of freedom. This was 'my time'. Sameer was on duty in the paediatric ward just like me the night before. I liked being with him. Our friendship went a long way. We had done our schooling and MBBS together. I rushed off to meet him.

'Why don't you guys ever come on call?' I complained. As paediatricians they rarely attended the deliveries.

'Your ward *bai* just slips the call letter under the door of our duty room and walks away without informing us.' He retorted.

I scowled at him. That was a blatant lie.

'Let's have tea.' He suggested.

'I am hungry too.' I said hopping behind on his scooter. We went off to have hot jalebis and samosas, our favourite breakfast, before he dropped me off at the hostel and rode off. Even he needed to be back in the wards soon.

I had promised to meet Sameer in the nursery. He was posted there along with a senior, Dr Ranjan who was a great friend too. He had joined post-graduation in paediatrics in our hospital more than a year back and was a very kind and helpful person. I really looked forward to seeing them both.

So, I went there a week later, on the pretext of checking up on a baby in the nursery whom we had delivered a couple of days back.

'Hello! So nice to see you here.' I said, greeting them.

'Where's your travelling bag?' Dr Ranjan never missed a chance to pull my leg. And he never missed asking about the kit, too.

Sameer laughed.

'Why, Sir? Don't tell me you too want something from the kit.'

'No, no. I just want to have samosas.' He, like most hostellers, was perennially hungry.

As we got down to our silly talks which were usually irrelevant, suddenly there was sound of approaching footsteps.

'Looks like Dr Ramani is coming for rounds.' Sameer said.

Dr Ramani was their senior lecturer and a close friend of my boss too. He would be the first one to report that her gynae girls were gossiping with his paediatric boys, that too in the wards. They were both very conservative and it wouldn't go down well with either.

'You go and hide in the terrace.' Dr Ranjan suggested. The only problem was that there was no door to the terrace. The only thing that connected the terrace to the ward was a small window. It was actually a parapet.

'Go, jump over it.' Dr Ranjan egged me on.

'Fast, Ramani is almost here.' Sameer peered from the door. They hardly gave me any time to ponder. Just acting on my instincts I climbed over the table and jumped out of the window on to the terrace, and right at that moment Dr Ramani walked inside.

Dr Ranjan rushed after him awkwardly, darting backward glances and Sameer followed suit staring obliquely at the terrace.

I landed with a thud on the terrace. It overlooked the front of the hospital. Almost everyone who entered the hospital could very easily spot me there, if they cared to look high enough. Fortunately, they didn't because this was the second floor. Yet, I was conscious and embarrassed too. It was now 30 minutes. How long could I just sit down and be invisible to all? There was no shade and the strong sun wasn't letting me sit in peace anywhere. I peered inside. The round was still on. At any other time I would have called this funny. Me, hiding on the terrace! Why the hell did I get pushed into this? I was not ever going to come to meet these stupid guys again. I fretted and fumed for another 20 minutes before relief arrived.

'You can jump back.' Sameer grinned from inside.

'Of all the foolish things in the world...' My voice trailed off as I landed into the nursery.

The two guys I called my friends, were rolling with laughter.

'Now listen. Yeah, yeah, it's funny.' I couldn't help joining them in laughter. 'Okay, but just don't tell anyone about this, right?'

They could barely manage nodding their head between their bouts of hysterical laughter.

'Now, let's go out for the samosas, before your boss comes. And this time I shall push both of you on the terrace.' I threatened them.

But to my chagrin they laughed more. That just reminded me to stay away from the nursery and its wayward doctors in future.

After that day, every time I entered the hospital I always remembered to glance upwards at the terrace on the second floor. Just in case!

One news that invoked much hostility was any of the postgraduates of our batch getting married. If you got married in the first-year PG, then the probability of going on maternity leave was imminent. To the other residents this was an impending disaster. Not that we were prejudiced, but in a resources-starved hospital with no provision of taking another ad-hoc resident, the extra responsibility would be borne by us.

The pregnant ones tired very easily. Even the patients looked at them with empathy. A call from the wards and of course they would look at you expectantly. They were by default exempted from such calls. But yeah, a surgery would never be out of bounds for them. Surgery was that prized possession nobody wanted to give away despite everything. So while you did all their clerical stuff, they would do all the clinical ones. No wonder we detested the moment any of our residents got married.

Their reluctance to move sometimes landed them up in hilarious situations. My pregnant senior, Namita, found herself in one.

One emergency night she waited for the radiologist for a transvaginal ultrasound on a patient of incomplete abortion. The probe had to be covered by a condom before it was put inside the vagina. But, predictably, the radiologist arrived without one.

The delay and the prospect of going to the wards to fetch a condom irked her.

'Why didn't you come with a condom?' She lashed out at the radiologist.

'I don't move around in the middle of night carrying condoms in my pocket.' The radiologist gave back just as ferociously.

It was the chuckling sounds that stopped the exchange from flaring up.

But not all marriages followed the predictable pattern.

Meera had got married few weeks back. It was an arranged marriage. She had been in a strange mood since her engagement. Couple of months back her father had called her home. That day she had met Tarun. His parents had a nursing home and he was an orthopaedic surgeon. It was a match made in heaven. They got engaged the very next day, and a starry-eyed Meera returned, wearing her heart on her sleeves. She could be seen hanging around the solitary telephone in the hostel, or waiting for his visit. Strangely, the calls were few and the visits none. On a few occasions that he promised to come, he didn't bother to turn up. No apology, no explanations! Strange behaviour indeed from a recently engaged guy.

However, the eyes conveniently ignore what the mind doesn't want to see. She learned to live through his indifference, convincing herself that not all guys were demonstrative. Love ignores and forgives too. She got married a few months later.

Her marriage was a typical Punjabi affair. A youthful, 23-year-old waited for him on her wedding night, with dreamy eyes. However, her inscrutable groom continued chatting with his brother's wife all night. She was fast asleep when he came back in the early hours of the morning. She woke with a start when he entered.

'I am tired,' he said brusquely, and turned his back.

'That was supposed to be my line,' she thought humorously, before going back to sleep again.

She played the adoring wife and, he, the aloof husband; always finding a reason to stay away. Thankfully, they were soon on their honeymoon. She was happy to be out with him alone at last, away from the 'omnipresent' *brother's wife*. Maybe she was getting jealous, but he was always attentive to his much older, and more beautiful, sister-in-law.

Her honeymoon was a bigger disaster than she could ever imagine. Her husband never showed any inclination to come close to her. Every advance by her was scorned. If she tried to broach the subject, he would admonish her for being a 'one-track mind'. She was getting confused and upset. With a heavy heart and a suspicious mind, she returned home with him. Something was definitely wrong.

On coming back, Tarun plainly told her that it couldn't work between them and she should leave. They called a cab for her, and in a haze she left home, leaving behind everything that was once precious to her, including her belongings. Her parents were shocked. They tried to mediate, but when her husband sneered about how unattractive Meera was and how she failed to turn him on, they gave up.

Meera's life plunged into darkness. A smart and intelligent doctor went on to buy books on personality development. Her repeated attempts at reconciliation were thwarted at every step by her hostile husband. It started affecting her professional life, too. She was hell-bent on putting everything on stake for him, and he never tired of ridiculing and destroying everything for her.

She had indeed touched upon the lowest point of her life.

'It's time you met a counsellor.' She was advised by her friends.

Finally, one day, she decided to see a counsellor. Of course, her husband refused to go along with her. They met the doctor, separately. She got a call from the doctor the very next day.

'Move out of this marriage. He is a destructive man.' It finally dawned on her that he was an insecure man hiding behind his own incompetence. She had wasted her life and career on an impotent man who refused to accept it. He didn't give her an easy divorce, either.

The telephone placed in the corner of the labour room was ringing sharply. There was no one around. Sighing, I rose from my chair to pick it up.

'Hello.'

'Do you have a clitoris?'

'What!'

The crude voice reiterated the sentence. A chill ran down my spine. Was I being stalked? I looked around. I couldn't see anyone. There were so many ghost calls these days in the labour room. There would be a string of obscenities but, strangely, only when picked up by a female doctor. In the last duty also a crude voice, almost in an illiterate tone, had used medical terms, pertaining to the female anatomy with so much vulgarity that I shuddered. Someone inside the hospital was a pervert.

Those days, the story of Aruna Shanbaug was much in news.

Just a couple of days back I had met this pathetic ward boy. Whilst on a round to the nursery where I had gone to take out some perinatal statistics for our academic meeting, I had suddenly looked up and found him blocking my way. He was looking obliquely at me covering one side of his face with his hands. He looked dirty and a little sick.

I asked him in an authoritative tone, '*Kya kaam hai* (What do you want)?'

He just looked at me in a creepy way and slowly took out a crumpled piece of paper from the pocket of his trousers. Not understanding much of what was happening, I opened the paper. There was only one word written—'*Nirodh.*' I cringed. My intuitions were ringing warning bells. How dare he!

I flared up with anger. Needing a physical outlet for the sheer disgust I was feeling, I started punching him. He shielded himself even as he grovelled. Hitting him, I hurt myself, too, but nothing could stop me. Instead of fear, there was a sick gaze in his eyes as he looked at me as if he was relishing every blow. That enraged me further.

I dragged him to the post-natal ward where the senior nurse, Sister Bhalla was sitting. She scolded him but the pathetic creature kept on covering his eyes and tilting his face. Bereft of all energy, I didn't know what to do with him. I left him with the ward nurse and called up my friends. They rushed to the ward. I was almost in tears. They took him away. He was roughened up in the boys' hostel thoroughly before being reported to the medical superintendent.

I put the phone down.

It rang again. I asked my male colleague, Dr Anuj to pick it up this time.

'Hello.' The voice on the other side went silent.

The phone was hung with a definite click.

This was getting worse. We needed to report this to the administration.

The other ward boy had not been expelled but was moved to the male ward in another building. I was relieved, though still uneasy with him being around. I wanted a more severe punishment but, according to the authorities, his crime was not very big. There were strong unions and the administration was wary of messing with them. Could he be the person behind the vulgar calls made to the labour room? My friends chided me for being a namby-pamby. They reassured me that he would never come near me again and I tried my best to get convinced. The days that followed showed no trace of him and, slowly I let go of my fears.

But then I met him again.

I had barely entered my duty room. After a long time there was some time to relax in the afternoon. I yawned. But before I could stretch a little, there was a knock on the door. And before I could even get down from the bed, he entered the room.

All colour drained from my face.

'What the hell are you doing here?' I screamed. He was cowering with his hand covering his face in that same sick manner. Bile rose in my throat.

'They sent me with this.' Once again he pulled out a piece of paper.

I snatched the paper from his hands.

It was a call from the medicine department to see a patient in the medical ward.

'Why did you come to my duty room? You were told not be seen anywhere near this department.' The mere sight of him was enough to fill me with revulsion.

'They sent me here with this call.' He wheedled and I cringed.

I was sure no one would ever send a ward boy to our duty room.

'Get out of here and next time if you are anywhere around here, I shall beat the life out of you.'

I was seriously thinking of reporting him to the police.

'Madam...' he croaked and faltered.

'Get out!' I didn't know where I was getting the strength to even talk to him.

He took his cue and disappeared. The peace of the day was broken and along with that my sense of security.

In a hospital as big as ours it was difficult to weed out such perverts who grew covertly in the dark corridors and lonely stretches of the premises.

I couldn't sit alone in the duty room any longer. I went back to the labour room and called up Sameer and Kavya. They listened to me with concern.

'Let's report to the MS tomorrow,' Kavya said.

'But what will you report?' Sameer said matter-of-factly.

'Why couldn't they keep him out of our hospital?'

Was it too much to expect from the administration? Was our safety not their concern? I felt watched and that was not a comfortable feeling to work with.

Fortunately, I didn't get much time to agonise over it.

A woman wearing a bright-red saree flanked by policewomen on either side walked into the labour room. A medico-legal case again!

'She was caught red handed with some famous and rich businessmen. The neighbours were suspicious about dubious activities going on and had reported to us. We have brought her here for check-up.' One of the policewomen informed us. The woman had been arrested from a posh locality in the city.

We were wary of these medico-legal cases. My memory was still raw with my recent rendezvous in the court for a rape victim where I had been slaughtered by the defence lawyer. As doctors working in government hospital, we often saw women who were brought for examination after rape. I remembered this traumatised woman as the one with frozen eyes. As I examined her, I noted an intact hymen. The hymen didn't necessarily go away always with intercourse. But in those days the definition of rape was different. Like in the Aruna Shanbaug case, the court noted that she was menstruating at that time and her rapist was charged with sodomy and not rape and let off with a lighter punishment.

I didn't need a judge to tell me that she had been victimised, but as a doctor I could not fight her case.

I could only state the facts. I had my limitation as a witness and the defence lawyer didn't take much time in unnerving me. Thinking objectively it was the prosecution who had failed to rise to the challenge. But the regret stayed because it was my testimony that went against the victim.

I had promised myself never to be in a courtroom again. But then how could you escape your destiny.

I looked at the present case. The woman was of short stature, married with three children, all caesarean deliveries. Even if there was no charge of rape yet the procedure followed was generally similar. As we got about taking slides and vaginal swabs, we discovered her vagina was very narrow.

'No wonder she had caesarean deliveries,' I said.

'*Arrey* Ma'am, imagine how she got pregnant!' Sneered our ward *bai* with her infamous dialogue. This was their favourite.

They would throw it at a woman whenever she got uncooperative during a vaginal examination. Labour rooms were known for these snide remarks too.

'*Doctoron ko dikhwaoge nahi, aadmi ko toh mana nahi kiya hoga* (You have reservations to allow the doctor to probe but never say no to your husband)!' The poor women would turn red and so would majority of us postgraduates. Later we learned to turn a deaf ear to them.

But it was not the laughter of the nurses and the ward *bai* that got to us. The woman was also laughing along with them. We stared at her. Tomorrow, once charged, she would cry rape! How easily people played with law. The majority who suffered went unreported whereas the minority who reported, faked it. But as doctors we were helpless.

At a time when majority reports went as 'rape could be verified only after chemical analysis', some cases went beyond case reports and shook your conscience.

Like a six-year-old girl who had come bleeding with severe injuries. She had been rescued from the roadside. Abducted and raped by her own neighbour, it was just as painful for the doctors even to touch her. The ordeal had scarred not only her but the entire society.

It was in these cases that you wanted to write in bold, 'rape had been committed beyond any doubt'. Yet, law had to take its own course.

It was not that we didn't see fabricated ones. It was a sad reality that laws were sometimes used to settle scores and avenge personal enmities especially between two villages.

'I was sleeping on the terrace when two guys crossed the roof from the neighbour's house and raped me!' claimed a girl brought by the police.

'What were you doing on the terrace all alone at night?' One of our PG who was also from a village asked her sternly.

Once inside the examination room, the alleged 'victim' confessed that she had been asked by her father to implicate the two men from the neighbouring village.

Who were we to judge women? That was for the courts to do. But be it true or fabricated, it was a woman who got exploited for sure.

With the swabs and slides ready and clothes sealed, we kept them in the cupboard inside the labour room. It would be handed over in the office tomorrow. The MLC (Medico-legal Certificate) register was also kept inside. Surprisingly the cupboard had no lockers.

'Madam, I need to talk to you.' I was surprised to see the ward *bai* of the post-natal ward standing in front of me.

'What happened?' I was wary of the staff.

Just two days back, while I was about to wind off, another staff had brought her daughter-in-law for check up. She was pregnant for the fourth time and looked pale.

'Why don't you people understand? *Mar jaogi bachche paida karte karte* (You will die giving birth to kids)!' I had said, exasperated.

Next morning, as I reported in the labour room, I was informed about her demise. It shocked me to the roots.

'Just once in a day, what you utter might come true. So always be careful.' It was an old wisdom that my mother often said.

I didn't quite believe in prophecy but it was so difficult to shrug off this feeling of guilt that washed over me.

'Madam, my son has been implicated in a rape case.' The voice of the ward *bai* broke through my reverie.

'The victim was brought here for medical examination. Please help me,' she requested.

Her intent in seeking me out was obvious.

'Everything has been sealed and sent to the office.' Refusals didn't have to be harsh especially when you were facing criminals. We were becoming expert at being diplomatic.

While today documents kept locked as 'soft copies' with passwords in a computer are still in danger of getting hacked, it's unbelievable how a frail cupboard without a single lock kept all our secret and legal documents safe.

With every passing day we were growing a little smarter. I recalled fondly the first caesarean where I had run away, in my final year.

Now, I had assisted in innumerable cases of caesareans. Just a few times I had also closed the abdomen. A house surgeon's job was generally about being a second assistant. We had to make sure everything was in place in the house. From the sutures, to drugs, to the dressing, everything had to be there before the surgery started.

'Why do we have to work as assistants to the anaesthetists?' Dr Anuj sounded pissed off.

'It's insulting.' I agreed.

'Keeping the oxytocin drip ready, the methergin vial open and filled in a syringe and kept on the Boyle's apparatus, isn't that supposed to be their work?' Dr Anuj exclaimed. 'I forgot to keep the filled syringe with the needle inside the broken vial for identification. You should have seen the ruckus they created!'

Now I knew why Dr Anuj was peeved.

'You are right. Even the anaesthesia house physician who is otherwise our batchmate, waits for us to break the vials else he will walk out smugly.' I said. Nothing rubbed our prestige more than this!

'It's bad for our self esteem. Yet, we have to carry forward this decadent practice.' Dr Anuj sighed.

As a house surgeon it was a matter of prestige to be the first assistant and we rejoiced whenever we got the opportunity.

'Ah, when do I get to be the operating surgeon?' My heart looked forward with excitement at the prospect of being the surgeon rather than the assistant. But there was no hurry. 'The right time will come and in all glory I will take out the baby myself and then stitch the uterus back in place.' I promised myself.

It was an emergency case that coincidentally made me the first assistant and even more! There was a breech delivery in the labour room and the second-year PG was left in the labour room while I was called to the operation theatre. The operating surgeon, Dr Mala was a little lost. Her mind was stuck with the breech delivery and she could not focus on the job at hand. These deliveries were always complicated. Being the senior-most person who reported to the head of department, she was apprehensive.

We were half way through the caesarean, the baby was barely out when the ward *bai* from the labour room came rushing.

'Madam, the trunk has delivered but the head is arrested inside. The RSO has asked for you to come immediately.' The *bai* said in a hurry.

Dr Mala's face paled. By now I knew enough to understand that it was pretty serious.

She immediately took off her gloves.

'Please finish the surgery with the nurse.' I gave a start! Me, all alone?

I just kept gaping at her as she rushed out without wasting a single minute.

I stared at the nurse. She looked back blankly. She was a senior nurse and had been working for more than ten years. And, I, who had been here for just a couple of months had to finish the surgery! Tentatively I took the first stitch. There, it felt almost easy!

'Am I doing it right?' I looked hopefully at the nurse.

'I can't comment, Doctor.' Came the brusque reply.

She didn't want to take any responsibility in case of any eventuality. I hesitated but I knew we couldn't wait forever for my senior to return.

Initially a little hesitantly and then a little boldly I finished the two layers of the uterus. I recalled my steps. Count the sponges and close the abdomen. Start with the peritoneum (innermost layer), rectus muscle and then the sheath covering the muscles. I was almost done with the rectus sheath when my senior returned.

'Everything alright in the labour room?' I asked about the breech delivery.

'We could pull it out. A little delayed cry, but the baby looks fine.' She sounded relieved.

She scrubbed and joined me again.

'You seem to have done a good job. I am sorry but I just didn't have any time to think about you.' She murmured appreciatively.

'Can you just check?' I hesitated. I wanted to be sure before we finally closed the patient.

She laughed. 'No need to reopen again. It looks fine.'

In all my heart I wished I could reciprocate the confidence.

'Isn't it, Sister?'

The nurse didn't say anything, just nodded.

Probably she had more confidence on the nurse than me. But it did make me feel better. My first closure and that too independently! That was no mean achievement.

'Be ready tomorrow. We shall celebrate it.' She smiled.

Of course! It was customary to celebrate the first innings, anywhere!

If the first abdominal closure happened to me much sooner than expected, the first caesarean took time. It was much later in my house job that I got to do my first caesarean.

The thrill of cutting open the abdomen, then the uterus and then putting your hand inside the uterus, below the head of the baby and gently scoop it out was extra ordinary. The sound of the baby as it let out its first cry filled me with a strange elation. As we cut the cord and handed over the baby to the paediatrician, nothing could dampen my enthusiasm. I had fallen in love, pure and profuse, with surgery.

My hands that closed the uterus and then the abdomen were more deft now. But as I came to stitching the skin, my senior said, 'Let's close it with a subcuticular stitch.'

That was a brilliant idea. After all, the scar was a surgeon's autograph. And I wanted it to look perfect.

I went on giving my first caesarean that perfect scar.

Unfortunately, it didn't heal that well. We catered to a population which didn't have the best standards of hygiene and neither was our hospital a state-of-the-art one, yet it hurt me more than her. I understood how possessive we were of our surgeries, they were our handiwork.

Surgery grows on you like an addiction and you crave to do more. I wanted to perfect the art. Every emergency day I would secretly hope to do a caesarean but then many of them passed with frustration. We now had senior residents in our department. They were the ones who had joined after their post-graduation for further training and grabbed most surgeries with both hands. We were being left frustrated.

To an extent I understood them but largely I didn't. The unfairness hurt but who said life was fair!

It was a very significant day for us. After extensively searching the libraries, attending many gruelling sessions and conducting researches, we were finally allotted our respective thesis topics. I was much happy with mine. I had collected enough literature on this topic:

'Rising rate of caesarean sections and its effect on maternal and perinatal mortality and morbidity.'

It was a very relevant topic and though it would mean lot of leafing through the files and shuffling the registers, I was happy. I would need to go to the records and do a lot of retrospective analysis and statistical work. I actually loved doing that.

Kavya was going to work upon, 'Hysteroscopy in infertility'.

We were allotted our thesis guides. Both of us were going to work under Dr Batra. We set about working on our theses and collecting data.

A few months later we found Parul sitting in the post-natal ward looking pensive. Kavya and I had gone there to collect the delivery register.

She was working on, 'Oxidative stress and DNA damage in male infertility'.

'But we don't deal with male patients, Parul.' I had been a little apprehensive about this topic.

'Infertility is a couple's problem, not just a woman's. And as gynaecologists we should not shy away from treating male infertility.' Her thesis guide, Dr Bali had countered. She had a point.

'So what's the problem now, Parul?' I asked her.

'I am not getting samples.' She informed sullenly.

'But infertility was so frequently seen in the outdoor clinics.' I countered.

'True, semen analysis is done routinely in most of these patients. It should not be difficult to get a sample.' Kavya said thoughtfully.

'Actually that's not a problem,' Parul said.

'Then?' I asked.

'I need controls to compare the infertile ones. I need semen from normal men.' Parul explained.

'How do you get normal men?' Kavya asked, clearly baffled.

'*Arrey*, normal men are those of proven fertility, like husbands of our pregnant patients,' Parul told us.

'Then take it from them.' We still didn't understand the problem.

'As if it was so easy!' Parul scowled.

We laughed. It was dawning on us.

'Dr Bali said that I should speak to the husbands of our delivered patients and motivate them to give their semen. They would serve as my controls.'

That sounded like a bright idea.

'So what's the hitch?' I asked.

'I have been trying my luck for so many months. But not a single sample has come my way. Do you know how embarrassing it has been? First, I look for the husbands, then take them to the doctor's room, explain to them about my thesis while they look at me blankly.' We laughed heartily as Parul narrated her experience.

'And then I have to brag about their "potent sperms" and that I would need them to compare with the less fortunate men.' Parul added.

We were now understanding her predicament.

'Initially I used to be very embarrassed. I would hesitate a lot but gradually I learned to ask for it without batting an eyelid.' Parul spoke dramatically.

'But even four months later, I have yet to get a single sample,' she almost cried.

'Why didn't you tell Dr Bali?' Kavya asked her.

'I did. She thought I was not asking the men properly, so one day she came along with me to explain to these husbands.' She spoke scathingly. 'Still no "husband" relented. Not a single willing husband!' She raised her hands in the air. 'What will happen to my thesis?'

'May be you are not motivating them enough.' I looked at her suggestively and she gave a troubled laugh. I really prayed she could somehow fix it and start her thesis work.

A few days later I found Parul in a much lighter mood.

'Hey, you managed to catch hold of a husband?' I winked at her.

'No, I don't need to any longer.' She grinned, crossing her heart.

'Why?'

'We found a way out. Dr Bali suggested that I collect all the semen samples that were reported normal from the laboratory. They would serve as my controls. Now I bring them all from the lab, and do my testing here.'

'That's awesome!' We were happy for her.

'But there's another problem,' she said.

'Now what?'

'I can't get rid of that smell. It just clings onto me. From my cupboard to everywhere that I go, that fishy smell follows me.' She admitted ruefully.

I sniffed. 'You are right. There's something fishy going on here.' Parul raised a playful fist and we all burst out laughing.

Indeed! I hoped her family didn't start smelling anything fishy too.

The cold vibes between the couple was very much palpable as they sat in the outdoor clinic.

'Madam, I delivered here three years back,' the woman said.

'So what brings you here again?' I asked.

'Actually it's my husband who has a complaint.'

I had no clue what she was leading to.

She raised her red-shot eyes towards him and said accusingly, 'He found a condom in the dustbin yesterday and thinks I am having an affair.'

Her husband looked troubled.

'Why can't you believe her?' The woman inside me leapt to her defence.

'I want to, honestly I do. But my daughter keeps telling me of this uncle who gives her chocolates,' the man replied.

'She's just a child.' The wife broke into a fresh round of sobbing.

'I always find her chatting with people on the phone, even late at night.'

'I am just doing my job.' She replied defensively.

'I don't want to destroy my marriage.' He looked equally tortured.

Still unmarried, I was not sure how to convince them.

'There is no gynaecological check up that can prove her innocence. No test can ever replace eroded trust.' Parul's voice broke in.

After a little lecture on love and trust, faithfulness and togetherness, we sent them off to a counsellor.

'Now we are detectives too.' Parul raised her eyebrows.

The next case in the clinic was an infertility patient and my interest was roused.

He was a young dentist and stood on the stool next to his wife. Taking out a small piece of paper, he pressed it forward.

'I can't speak out all that troubles me. So I have written everything on this paper,' he said.

That small piece spoke volumes. It read, 'I have been married for three months and I have had sex 100–120 times with my wife.' I paused. So many times and why was he counting? I continued reading. He had written that he had more than 800 complaints against his wife.

'Because of trying so many times I have developed blisters. I tried to put Lacto Calamine over it but it doesn't come down. I am scared I have developed an STD (sexually transmitted disease). And all that is because of her.' He sat quietly while we read.

'I feel something pricking me when I am inside her. I want you to find out if she has a Copper-T inserted or maybe it's something else to hurt me. I also want to tell you that she has grey hair there. That's a big turn off to me. And she has bad odour from her mouth as well. That again is a big turn off.' The rantings went on endlessly, mostly irrelevant.

The wife was examined and nothing was abnormal. All her reports also came out normal. She worked in an IT company and looked well educated. The poor woman didn't have a single word to say against her husband. Theirs was an arranged marriage and they had not been able to conceive.

'There is nothing apparently wrong about her. You still need to give your sample.' I told the dentist.

He was obviously reluctant. 'I am not the one with problems. I don't even suffer from any chronic disease.'

He had no choice but to comply.

I met Parul in the wards later in the afternoon.

'I have sent a sample for you. Let me know about him.' I told her everything about that strange slip of complaints.

A few days later Parul came rushing to me and exclaimed.

'What a wonderful sample you arranged for me.' I raised my eyebrows.

'It was all urine.'

We burst out laughing. Now we understood why.

'He's such a smart guy, shielding behind her when all the time he was the one with a problem.'

'By the way did you tell him the report?'

'I told him that it was all urine and he was like "why can't you retrieve the sperms from the urine?" He was so defiant!' Parul said.

The psyche of some men, always trying to put the blame on their wives, even for their own incompetency!

Maybe he was impotent or suffered from retrograde ejaculation. We never could find out for he didn't return.

Meanwhile, Kavya was trying hard to motivate a woman for hysteroscopy. The patient had failed to conceive inspite of being married for about five years. Kavya was about to take her consent for hysteroscopy, when Parul came rushing down.

'Her husband has zero sperm count. No point investigating her.'

The young woman had to be counselled, but before that her father-in-law stepped in with a solution. He had heard Parul.

'I can donate sperms to her.' We gaped at him. Too embarrassed to say anything we took him to our professor who was sitting in the next room. If she was shocked, she didn't show it.

'It's impossible, we don't allow semen donations from relatives.' However, he kept on insisting. There was no way one could even listen to such an indecent proposal.

'Parul, since you started working on your thesis, we have been flooded with weird patients.' I said.

'I stand guilty.' She accepted ruefully.

A few months later the same woman came back, distraught. Not put off by our refusal to inseminate her with his sperms, her father-in-law had taken a different recourse.

'He keeps pestering me. He will drop hints that he has not named the property to any of his children. He forces me to visit him daily in the evening.' She said between sobs. The implication was obvious and repugnant. Even her husband and her mother-in-law kept quiet despite being aware of all the atrocities. She could report him but without any support, clearly lacked the nerve.

'I feel so guilty and ashamed of myself. And where would I go after this?' She cried earnestly.

Despite endless debate, none of us came up with any sensible solution.

'I would have castrated him.' Parul spoke through gritted teeth. 'I should do a thesis on these kinds of men!'

If only wishes were horses, beggars might ride.

'Get some blood for her, fast!' My senior said, her voice tense.

Though I loved surgery yet there were times I wished I was anywhere else.

A young woman had been taken up for a caesarean. But once the baby was out, the patient started to bleed.

'Keep the oxytocin running.' The anaesthetist complied. He had secured another access to her veins and was keeping the fluids going fast along with the medicines.

'I think you should descrub and send an ambulance for the consultant on duty.' Came the anxious voice of my senior.

I called up Dr Batra. She lived in the campus and didn't even wait for the ambulance.

By the time she reached, the decision to remove the uterus had been taken. The patient was losing a lot of blood from there. It had not been easy explaining it to the attendants either. Acceptance is low when a negative outcome is least accepted.

Meanwhile, I rushed our intern to the blood bank and got blood released fast.

Unfortunately, even with the uterus removed, the patient kept on bleeding. Dr Batra was trying hard to maintain some semblance to the tissues but failed.

'I think we should inform Dr Bali.' Dr Bali was the senior most in the unit.

I tried her number many times but everytime it went unanswered.

The bleeding was getting critical.

'We shall have to do an internal iliac artery ligation and stop the blood supply to this area. I need help in doing that.' Dr Batra looked worried. 'Why don't we call the professor? After all, she is the head of department.'

That sounded simple and sensible. I immediately rang her up and briefed her up about the patient.

'Where is Dr Bali?' She asked.

'Ma'am, she is unreachable.' I said.

'How irresponsible!' I kept quiet. She was talking about my teacher. I could hardly affirm or negate that.

'Ask Dr Batra to send me a written call.' I conveyed this.

Dr Batra got incensed.

'Tell her, I can't leave the patient to write a call.' She shouted. She was almost sweating.

I tuned pale. I could hardly speak to my professor like that. I put down the phone.

'It's more sensible to call a surgeon.' The anaesthetist chipped in.

Dr SK Jain, the surgeon, lived in the campus and was in the operation theatre within minutes.

Calm prevailed in the theatre as soon as he entered. He went on to do the ligation of the internal iliac artery and within minutes the tissues stopped bleeding.

I had never admired a person more. Not only had he saved the patient, he had literally sailed us out of a very tricky situation.

He had barely ligated the offending vessels when the professor entered. Since I was the only person who was not scrubbed in the surgery, I was left to face a barrage of words.

'It's not my call day. How can I come till I do not get a written call?' She said angrily.

I nodded. There was little else I could do. After checking that the patient was stable, she left.

I thanked my stars that I was merely a resident. If this is what happened when you get senior I wished to remain a junior forever.

Sameer was in his paediatric ward. Minus the *ho-hallaah* so characteristic of gynaecology department, their wards always felt much too peaceful. Sameer and I went back so many years. The easy familiarity showed. We were too comfortable with each other.

'I think Sameer keeps staring at you.' Back in fourth year once a friend of mine had teased.

'Shut up! He's almost like a family to us.' My best friend, Kavya sprang to my defence. It was true. Even my parents knew him well. He was a frequent visitor to our place.

Apart from Kavya, Sameer, Varun and Raj, we were a gang of around ten friends. To our families, we were friends who had become doctors together, but to us it went much beyond, much deeper. We were those who had spent life's most imperfect moments together. And it were those moments that we cherished the most, they made our most beautiful memories.

If some memories brought nostalgia, some brought embarrassment.

Like that time when we had gone to a new hotel to celebrate Raj's birthday. We soon got so absorbed in ourselves that we forgot all orientation to time and place until we were rudely interrupted by the waiter.

'Can you all please keep the volume low? The other customers are complaining, we might have to ask you to move out.'

Were we really being threatened to be thrown out because we were rowdy? That made us throw more raptures of laughter. It was Raj who was most sober though he laughed the wildest. Few more fits of laughter, few more snide remarks by curious and angry onlookers, few more warnings by the hotel staff before the food arrived and common sense prevailed.

There were some moments that were not just embarrassing but they drove home a point too.

Like the time we were all returning from Delhi after our All India pre-PG entrance examination. The day after the exam was the most relaxing. Studies were forgotten and we allowed ourselves to go with the flow. We all took an overnight train. Travelling together was so much fun. A bunch of 15–20 students with no reservation, we chose to travel in a sleeper compartment.

I got down at Mathura to buy a packet of chips. While waiting for the change, I turned back and saw that the train had started moving. Forgetting my precious hundred rupee note, I ran back, scared to my roots. The train had started to pick speed and I had never boarded a moving train. As I reached near my coach, I found that Raj had actually got down for me. We couldn't board back ours but in the next coach two guys standing at the door pulled me up while Raj supported me from behind. This 'salvage' became historic. I really felt like a 'damsel in distress' and Raj was my 'knight in shining armour'. We spent some time in the other compartment before my heartbeat running in synchrony with the train, gradually slowed down. We moved back to a rousing welcome to our own coach when the train stopped at the next station. Raj became an undisputed hero, my saviour, and a lifetime friend.

High on adrenaline I could hardly sleep. There was a new boy, Saurabh in our group. He had shifted to our college to complete his internship. He was the kind who made the butterflies go wild in your tummy and he didn't look keen to sleep either. So we kept talking, all through the night, unmindful of people sleeping in our compartment. We talked about our likes and dislikes, giggling over silly things. It was almost dawn when we retired to our berths.

The sun rays filtered a new morning and I got down greeting my new friend. The magic of the night was over and I was feeling a little sheepish. Suddenly we heard voices.

'These boys and girls! They enter medical and then they grow old there. They won't get married at the right time and look what happens to them.' They spoke in crude Haryanvi, loud enough. The intent was obvious.

I turned red with embarrassment. Fortunately, my other friends were still sleeping.

Soon most of us had moved out of the city, pursuing post-graduation in our dream branches. The ones left behind got grilled in their hectic schedules. Sameer's paediatric department was in the same building. Initially I visited him with Kavya. Sameer was generally with his friend and senior Dr Ranjan. But gradually the pressure of 'duty' started taking a toll on our friendship. It was getting impossible for all of us to get free at the same time. Lately, Sameer and I were spending quite a lot of time with each other.

There was a strange flutter whenever I thought about him.

He was inserting a venflon when I reached his ward. He threw a careless smile at me, a smile that always lifted my spirits.

I moved to the doctors' room and waited for him. Earlier I used to feel a little uncomfortable alone with him. Strangely, I didn't anymore.

I smiled as he entered the room.

'It was such a difficult vein access.' Children usually had thin veins and paediatricians were the smartest in inserting intravenous lines.

'You guys are smart there.' I admitted.

'*Arrey* no. Show me your veins.' He said.

Surprised, I held out my hand. He traced a thin, long vein at the back of my hand.

'You have nice veins.'

He held my wrist and turned it. My heart skipped a beat. Outwardly, I tried to control an involuntary shiver.

'Come on, I am not fat! So, I will have nice veins.' I played it away.

Sameer laughed. I was once again touched by his boyish laughter. The deep rumbling sound broke the tension, reluctantly.

'Let's go and have tea.' It was a good idea to leave the ward. Soon, the charged atmosphere of the ward was replaced by the bonhomie of a tea stall.

The gastronomics of drowning romance down the drain! No wonder, I was wary of medicos. I had promised myself that if I ever married, it would be to a non-medico. But not all promises were meant to be kept!

The early days of residency were always unique. On one hand you carried the burden of the whole house on your head, silently condemning the seniors for leaving it all on to you; on the other hand, every time you were stuck in a crucial case you silently thanked your stars that there was someone above to take the responsibility.

I had hardly walked into the labour room when I found out that I was to be alone there once again. The rest of the team would be practically in the operation theatre as two surgeries had already been shifted and another was on the way.

A patient was in preterm labour. Her baby had died inside and was in breech presentation. I was a little apprehensive. I had never delivered a breech alone.

'Ma'am, don't worry. We will do it together.' The nurse looked at my frowning face and smiled.

'Thank you, Sister. They might get free in time.' I still couldn't help wishing.

The patient was soon fully dilated.

'It's a still birth.' The nurse tried to reassure me. At least I didn't have to worry about the baby.

The buttocks started showing. The nurse asked me to come close. Like in the dummy pelvis, I scooped out the buttocks and soon the baby was delivered till the trunk. I rotated the baby so that the back was upwards. The sister then gently hooked the shoulders and delivered both the arms. It was easy till now. Now the baby was hanging outside but the nape wasn't still visible.

'Don't pull much. The best thing is to let the baby hang by its own weight.' The nurse advised me.

She took out two IV bottles and tied them together with a tape gauze, and then tied them to the trunk of the baby and allowed them to hang hence dragging the baby downwards.

'You are so innovative, Sister!' I looked at her appreciatively.

'*Nahi*, Ma'am, even I learned everything here only, from my seniors.' She waved off my compliments graciously.

It took a couple of hours but we waited patiently. With pressure the baby was dragged down and soon the nape of the neck was visible. I could now pull the baby out. I looked at the nurse and she winked at me. This was my first breech delivery, under the guidance of my labour-room nurse.

But my problems were not over. Still births sometimes gave rise to problems like DIC (disseminated intravascular coagulation). Here the blood didn't clot and the patient kept on bleeding. I gave her medicines but the bleeding still refused to stop.

'I think we should pack her up, isn't it, Sister?' I valued her experience now. The nurse nodded.

I called up the consultant on call. It was past midnight and she appeared to be sleeping.

'Give her some methergin and oxytocin. She will stop bleeding. And rub her uterus into contraction.' She murmured sleepily before putting the phone down.

I had already tried all these. I had even arranged for blood. Sadly, there were no attendants and it was going to be a big trouble if the bleeding continued. To add to my woes her blood pressure started dropping.

'Ma'am, we need to pack her.' I informed the consultant, but she was not ready to listen.

'We shall see that in the morning.' She put down the phone.

I was aghast but my decision had been made. I asked the nurse to arrange for two tape gauzes and started packing the cavity of the uterus. I filled the uterus with a tape gauze, tightly in layers, one above the other. I kept another pack in the vagina. Miraculously, it worked! The uterine packing compressed the oozing sinuses and she stopped bleeding. Her BP started improving and soon I was able to go to the duty room and stretch my tired muscles.

In the morning by six, the team from the operation theatre returned, all drained out. It was eerie that at the same time when I was caught with a difficult breech delivery they were also doing a breech delivery, exactly stuck at the same points as me. Their challenge was tougher as there was a healthy baby, central to their concern.

They had been worried about me. I laughed and told them about my saviour and my guide that night.

One good deed deserves another. I returned to the labour room the next day with a box of chocolates for my teacher of the day, the labour-room nurse.

There was always a knight in the shining armour, sometimes a technique, sometimes a face waiting to be recognised. We had to reach forward and embrace it.

My consultant, whom I met the next day beamed, 'I knew you could do it'. I smiled. All is well that ends well.

'Are you post-duty?'

I hated this. Post-duty meant the day following your emergency night.

It implied I was looking hassled and tired when I had just arrived into the hospital and had barely started taking my rounds.

I had thick long tresses and I knew they attracted quite a few admiring glances. However, they kept coming out of places, at all times. Even while I tried my best to keep them under the head cap in the operation theatre, they would threaten to come out.

'Sister, will you please push that strand back under the cap of the doctor.' The anaesthetist would rudely remind me indirectly.

It didn't help in the labour room either when I had to push them back with my gloved hands during a delivery. I didn't want to risk soiling it with amniotic fluid.

It was not that people hated long hair for nothing. A loose strand of hair could risk infection to the patient, apart from being irksome when you were operating.

The only option left was to chop my hair. And I did just that. Sacrificed my hair at the altar of duty. I brushed away an imaginary tear in memory of my long tresses. Soldiers were sacrificing their lives at the front!

Of course, it had nothing to with the fact that Sameer liked short hair. And, of course, it was a mere coincidence that I saw him again that day.

'You look different.' At least he had noticed. Maybe I was shaking my small pony tail a little too obviously.

He kept looking me strangely then smiled.

'So you chopped off your hair? Suits you.' That was rich. You never expected compliments from Sameer. Be it a new dress or a new look, he never seemed to notice.

Anyway, I felt a little less guilty about cutting them off.

I went back to my ward and waited for Bani to turn up. She was posted with me in the antenatal ward. I wanted her to stay there so that I could go to the preoperative ward. I had been given the additional charge of both the wards which were adjacent to each other.

The preoperative ward was considered a very strategic place. All the patients who were to be posted for major surgery were admitted here. Each of our teachers had their fixed operating day and their patients had to be fit for surgery before that. An unfit patient invited unnecessary ire from the concerned consultant.

'Sister, when will Dr Bali come?' I asked the nurse.

'She would be a little late today.'

'Oh, I was waiting for her signatures on the requisitions for chest X-ray and ECG. How will I get the patients fit for surgery?'

'Don't you know what to do?' The nurse asked me.

I looked at her. Was it such a common knowledge?

'Don't worry, they all do it.' The nurse grinned.

I wasn't left with a choice either. It was already nine. I took out the requisitions and signed her name across in a signature that was almost identical to hers. The radiologist just wanted to see that '*chidiya*'. That's what we called their signatures. There, half my job was done now. I sent the patients happily for her tests.

Most of the consultants had a very easy signature. Now I understood the reason behind that.

If a consultant could do it, the residents could do it too. It was not forgery. This was patient care. We had no reason to feel guilty. Even the consultants were aware of it.

I was not worried anymore if Dr Bali came late for rounds.

But I was not the only one looking for someone.

'Is Dr Bali here?' Tushar, our intern, asked.

Why was he looking for Dr Bali? It was rather unusual. Since my posting in the antenatal ward I had found him many a times looking for her.

I shrugged off. He came from a medical background. He might be known to Dr Bali.

A few days later I was with Bani in our emergency duty. The labour room was busy, the staff rushed and patients were uncooperative. Enough to try a resident's patience!

It was around ten when I could walk out for my dinner break.

As I came back, I found Tushar again in the labour room. This time he didn't ask me about Dr Bali.

Bani was sitting on the bench while he sat on the armrest. There was nothing unusual about Tushar being in the labour room. Interns were always welcome in the labour room. What was odd was the way he sat so close to her, leaning a little suggestively as they whispered to each other.

I flushed a little guilty. He was our intern, much junior. I shouldn't even think like this. I went to take a little rest in the first half of the duty. He was still there when I came back.

This became a pattern. In almost every emergency duty that I had with Bani, Tushar was a constant presence. She always took a break in the second half of the night. And I would always come back from my break to find both of them together. Well, PDAs were not a norm in our medical college. And I felt a little embarrassed.

I couldn't help telling Sameer about them. He laughed.

'What's odd about it?' He asked as I stared back at him.

'They are a group of friends and we often spot her in the hostel too.' He said.

'But he's just an intern.' I countered.

'Come on, stop being so old fashioned about it.'

I was amazed at his matter-of-factness.

I should rather mind my own business and stop over thinking.

It was the annual functions that brought out Bani's notoriety and the extent of rumours going around in the hostel. Her sojourns with Tushar and his friends, her nocturnal visits to his hostel were being frequently noticed and talked about in the boys' hostel. The boys were in no mood to let it go.

They were in search of a *'bakra'* and who better than Bani? Not being from our college she had not many friends and was an easy target.

Bani was in labour room when the phone rang.

'Hello,' she answered.

'Is it Bani?'

'Yes.'

'Today you were looking so, so very beautiful.' The voice on the other side swooned, while the others covered their mouths to shut out the giggles.

'Who is this?'

'You didn't recognise me? The one with the orange shirt.' It was a made up thing.

'I think I saw you.' Bani said.

There was another round of stifled giggles.

'Your beauty is divine. Intoxicating like an old wine.' He was using all his power over prose to flatter her.

Bani smiled.

'Can you look at the roof above?' The caller said.

'Yes, I can.'

'I wish I could fly from here, break the roof and land at your feet.' The burst of laughter couldn't be contained any longer. The line then went dead.

Needless to say the boys had found a gullible target.

It was now past midnight. The phone rang again.

Bani answered.

'Congratulations!' It was a different voice this time.

'Who is this?' Bani asked.

'Madam, I am calling from Agra. You have been blessed with a baby brother.'

'What rubbish!' Bani slammed the phone down. The guys rolled on the floor with laughter.

'It is not fair.' Kavya looked sullen. Raj was having difficulty narrating it, his voice getting muffled and broken by the frequent bouts of laughter. He clutched at his stomach.

'This might be funny but not fair. Why should a girl be targeted and not the guys?' Kavya said.

'*Arrey,* you girls are welcome to target them. They would love it actually.' Raj winked.

Raj was now doing his post-graduation in orthopaedics and was posted in the JA Hospital that was at a little distance from ours. We met less frequently because of our busy schedules. His quiet and witty demeanour had found many admirers. His scooter was keenly followed by those in the girls' hostel.

But he was in trouble.

'I am being stalked!' he told us one day. We laughed.

'Guys, I am serious! Last week I had malaria and had to go for some blood tests. When I went to collect the reports, I was told they had already been picked up by someone.'

This was mysterious.

'Later, I received a phone call. I was told to collect the reports from *her* room.'

'Who's "her"?' I asked.

He hesitated. 'Actually, Dr Riya from medicine. She made around 50 calls and I had to go to her room.' Raj said.

'But isn't she the one whose marriage got fixed? I think she's already left for her hometown.' I said.

'Exactly! She was leaving the very next day. When I reached she first offered me a drink.'

'Oh! Really?' That brought a gasp from all of us. Riya had done MBBS with us but we never realised the extent of her infatuation.

'She then started cribbing why I never paid any attention to her and declared that she loved me.' Raj blurted out.

'Then?' We asked together.

'Then what? Guys, she literally assaulted me. She kept on repeating that this was going to be our last chance together. I had to actually run from her room.'

If it were not his troubled expression we would have laughed in disbelief.

'Come on, Raj. Don't you know we guys just fantasise about being in such a situation?' The light rejoinder from Varun broke the tension. Even Raj laughed.

'Now, next time any girl calls you, take any one of us along. We would love to swap places with you.' Varun said wickedly. It was good to see him laughing. He was finally himself, after days of recovering from a painful break-up.

'Girls, do you know Varun was planning to plant a bomb under the bed of his ex girlfriend last night?' Raj looked at him and then at us.

Varun grinned sheepishly.

'We made the programme around midnight.' A few drinks down and they had turned adventurous.

'We even hid below the car that was parked in front of her room in the hostel. It was just that the security guard refused to budge from his place so we were forced to give up.' Raj said.

'You guys are so stupid. You could have been rusticated.' I said.

All these years and we still couldn't make out whether they were serious or just making it all up.

I had barely changed inside the duty room that I saw Rashmi walk inside.

'Why did you leave the labour room?' I was surprised. Rashmi was a little lazy, and we were all aware of her habit of shirking work. But being her batchmate, scolding or disciplining her was out of my purview.

'I think they have deliberately paired you both.' Kavya said thoughtfully.

I was not happy to hear that.

'You both complement each other so amazingly.' She teased me.

'Don't worry, it is your turn next.' I gave her back.

All house surgeons were paired in rotation for emergency duty. Mine was the most unfortunate one, at least for the time being. Rashmi not only had an awful handwriting, she carried the most absurd and inconspicuous kits and depended on her partner for everything, from the kit to her share of clinical work. Her favourite pastime was undisputedly 'adjusting duties'.

Like a Rubik's cube, she could adjust even the most unlikely duty, out of a goblet of unseen possibilities. You name a duty and she could count it all on her fingertips and come up with a perfect solution.

And she was always planning her forthcoming holidays. She overstretched them, often taking medical leaves to compensate for the exhausted casual leaves.

No wonder her work efficiency suffered. She spent her time either having tea with the staff or giving orders to the juniors. Seniors rarely bothered with her. Nobody expected much from her and that was her strategy. No case presentations, hardly any worthwhile seminars, no lectures. Few could comprehend when she started speaking. It was not about the language but her content that got lost on people. Obviously she had the least responsibilities. Even our professor was wary of her.

It was just my bad luck. With her around there was no sharing of responsibilities. For all practical purposes I knew I was alone. Of course she was adept at arranging tea, snacks and gossips. There was no deficiency on her part there.

I had barely entered the labour room and taken over from our colleagues when a patient was brought inside.

'She seems to be having strong labour pains.' The nurse said as she made her lie down on the first labour bed.

'She is fully dilated and the presenting part is breech.' Rashmi announced.

It meant the baby was upside down and considering the contractions that she was having the baby would soon be out into the world.

'She is unbooked.' I looked worriedly at her lack of papers. There was no history of any check-ups done in the past either. 'How's the foetal heart beat?' I asked Rashmi.

'I can't find any,' she said.

That prompted me to spring to the patient's bed side. But despite trying hard I could not localise any heartbeat.

'It's not there.' Unfortunately this one was an intrauterine death of the foetus.

There was a sizeable population of such 'unbooked' patients visiting our hospital. A visit to a quack or a *dai* didn't constitute an antenatal visit and those who got referred from the *dais* were always high risk and generally ended up having complications. They were the ones who had been tried and tested and stretched beyond acceptable limits and then given up. They generally turned up after midnight. We called them 'train from Pakistan' blithely.

An 'intrauterine death' or IUD baby ruled out an operative delivery at this stage. Every effort would be made for a vaginal delivery in these cases. Moreover, this was the patient's third delivery and as such she had a good chance of a successful vaginal, breech delivery.

Still an informed consent about the IUD baby with all the implied consequences was to be taken. I wrote it in Hindi and Rashmi took the paper outside to get the consent from her attendants.

The patient progressed into labour very fast and it wasn't more than 15 minutes after her reaching the labour room that she delivered. The huge gush of fluid that followed was unusually golden stained.

'Ouch! I have soiled my clothes.' I exclaimed.

It fell directly on my dress.

'I am feeling uncomfortable. I think I shall have to go to the duty room.' I had no spare clothes which meant I had to clean the ones I was wearing.

Infection was a big concern especially when you had no clue about HIV and hepatitis status amongst the multitude of other infectious diseases that could get easily transmitted through the fluids. Meanwhile, Rashmi had just returned after taking the consent. She was very practical and smart in choosing the right moment to arrive.

'Can you just take care of the patient? I need to clean myself urgently.' I left the labour room upon her and moved to the duty room.

The golden flecks in the fluid lingered. Could this mean a post-dated pregnancy, Rh-negative pregnancy or one with jaundice? It was too early to comment. I tried to shrug off other possibilities. I would need to find out more from her attendants.

I had barely washed off the stains and was waiting for my dress to dry off when Rashmi walked inside the duty room.

'Why did you leave the labour room?' I was a little irritated and asked again.

'You unnecessarily stress a lot. There is nothing active in there. So I thought of relaxing a little,' she said casually.

With Rashmi, the other person became more responsible by default. I was probably overreacting.

She kept on talking about mundane issues. An hour had passed. I was clean and my clothes drier. We moved back to the labour room.

As soon as I entered the labour room I noticed something was amiss. It was unusually quiet. The patient who I had left behind was lying turned to one side.

Something drew me to her.

'Are you alright?' I asked.

As I went to turn her, I realised that she was not responding to any verbal commands. Intuitively, my hands moved to her pulse. I couldn't feel any!

'What happened, Sister?' I shouted.

'Nothing ma'am, she just slept after you left.' The nurse said.

I tried to revive her but failed. I was nonplussed and started asking the other interns and medical students posted there. But none of them had noted anything untoward. She was just resting after the delivery.

'No injections? Any drug that could have caused allergic reaction?' I asked.

'We didn't give any injections.' The nurses were not forthcoming either.

'But how could anyone die just like that?' I was staring at faceless people. Everyone looked away.

'Rashmi, did she bleed after I left?' I asked.

'No, of course not. Anyway, I was not here for long.' She averted her eyes, too ready to wash off her hands.

If it was difficult explaining to the attendants, it was more difficult reporting this death to the professor.

'Oh really?' That was all she said on the telephone.

The attendants denied any request for post-mortem. They quietly took the body and walked away from the hospital.

Next day it was all over the departments.

'These days residents keep sitting in the labour room and patients die mysteriously.' One of the senior medical officers commented sarcastically. Some people actually enjoyed issuing blanket statements and cast sweeping judgment on all and sundry.

All death case sheets had to be summarised in a death summary by the on-duty resident and this was presented in the death review meeting.

Soon, I was under the scanner in the death review meeting.

'So, what happened?' The professor asked. All eyes, including that of Rashmi were focussed on me. She behaved as if she was not even present there and was least answerable. What could I explain while I myself was searching for answers? I decided to be honest.

'Ma'am, she was an unbooked patient with no previous records. I had delivered the breech baby. It was still birth. I was almost drowned by her fluids. So I went to dry myself in the duty room.' I volunteered hesitantly.

'How much time do you take to change?' The professor asked.

'Ma'am, I had left the patient in Dr Rashmi's care.' Enough was enough!

Everyone looked at Rashmi. She averted their glance and again started looking at me, unperturbed. The futility of anything forthcoming from her was not lost on anyone.

'So, you mean the residents were changing clothes and the patient died in the labour room, of no known cause?' The professor jeered.

Others gave a snort of laughter. Some people really enjoyed other people's discomfiture. I was almost in tears.

It wasn't that there were no causes of sudden death. The *dai* could have ruptured her uterus before she referred her. I had offered the attendants post-mortem too. It was not my fault that they had refused.

'Embolism is not a very rare or unheard cause of sudden maternal death.' Kavya tried to console me.

Rather it was common. I knew that but how could I prove it?

Despite all my hard work and sincerity it was I who faced the heat. No questions were asked to Rashmi. Not a single one! That hurt.

If this was a cunning world, you were fighting all alone here. It was any day better to be alone than trust the calculating and incompetent people who leaned on you like parasites for their own survival. And they always had the easy way out. A priceless lesson learnt for life.

There were some days that were festive and some that were family days. However, they didn't necessarily happen together for the postgraduates. But Diwali and Holi were such festival times when even our professors got a little lenient with the residents, especially the hostellers.

'It's festival time, they have to go home. The day scholars must graciously do their duties.'

It was another matter that even the day scholars were hardly home, usually just in time for sleep. To our neighbours we were those creatures in white they saw early mornings and late evenings. The hostellers were still lucky. They would at least have some 'family time' away from the hospital.

So, festivals meant additional duties for those who were left behind. If the batch was lucky enough to have a non-Hindu resident gracious enough to do the festival night, the rest of the batch could celebrate Diwali night. The festival was divided into two parts, day and night.

This was my first Diwali at our new home. It had been almost eight months that we shifted and I was yet to see my new house swathed in bright sunshine. I looked forward to sitting in the terrace while listening to music or reading a book. That would remain an unfulfilled dream.

Diwali meant full 'day' duty, dash home just in time for the *puja* and then back the next day for a routine duty. The following day was always *Bhaidooj*—another festival but to us a full 24-hour emergency.

It was not easy leaving all festival preparations on your parents. Feeling guilty yet helpless, I promised my mother to be back home as early as possible and help her.

No sooner had I reached the hospital that I was told that two patients had already been shifted for caesarean. I rushed to the operation theatre on the first floor. There were two female attendants waiting outside, wearing colourful, festive clothes and jewellery. It filled the atmosphere with much gaiety and I appreciated the festive touch people brought to the otherwise bland hospitals. It definitely lifted my sombre mood. But strangely their faces looked sad.

I didn't have much time to dwell on that.

'Hello, keep this list for things that you need to bring for the surgery. We shall need them soon.' I told them.

Not that I wanted them to rush. But it was pointless to ask once the surgery was over. They never did. Some even insinuated that they were deliberately made to bring things that were already in stock. Ultimately it was the next patient in emergency who suffered.

Another hour later I came out of the OT to check if they had brought the sutures. For a house surgeon the foremost duty was to replenish the kit.

I saw the same woman, her head covered with a golden, *zari*-bordered, red saree sitting on the floor in a corner just outside the OT door. She was just staring into the space.

'Your patient and the baby both are fine.' I told her.

'Thank you, Sister.' She folded her hands in gratitude. I had learned to ignore the 'sister' part.

'Where's the list?' I asked cautiously. Our obsession with our kits refused to die. I had my depleting stores in mind.

She pulled back the saree from her head. In front of my stunned eyes she slowly unplugged her earring and held it out.

'We don't have any money. Can you please keep this and buy whatever you want to.'

I was bewildered.

'She is my sister. Today is Diwali but…' Her voice broke off as she started crying.

I felt almost morose.

'She's had a baby girl!' I couldn't help saying that. The news of a baby girl reduced some to tears.

'No, Laxmi*ji* has come to our house today. It's a good omen.' She said.

It was in situations like these, faced with the helplessness people lived with, that your own problems started looking petty. There I was, spoiling my mood over doing a festival emergency duty. I knew my parents would be proudly telling everyone about their daughter working on Diwali. And in all honesty, I would have just wasted my day lazing around rather than helping my mother with her chores.

'Keep your earrings.' I told her reassuringly.

She smiled shyly. My melancholy of the morning had strangely disappeared. My kit could wait, there were more important things in life. Like a pair of gold earrings in a poor woman's life. I smiled and went back into the operation theatre.

If Diwali in hospital was a little lonely, Holi was just the opposite. It was actually fun being in the campus. Once again majority of the hostellers went back to their hometowns; however, the ones who remained in the hostel and those on duty made sure they had fun. The duty would start with rubbing *gulal* over each other, the ward nurses and the staff. And, soon we took turns to visit our teachers. This was one time that we were allowed to move out officially on an unofficial sojourn. Holi was a day that somehow broke all inhibitions and all protocols. Duty and designation both were forgotten for a split second as both the junior doctors and the senior consultants rubbed *gulal* over each other.

But, before we stepped out of the hospital it was important to hear this story, more of a warning...

A couple of years back two RSOs from the labour room decided to pay the customary Holi visit to their teachers. Drunk in the festive colours and a generosity that such days imbibe, the teacher asked them to have some *laddus* and *thandai* before they left. Neither knowing, nor warned in all the bonhomie that followed, the two residents followed the delicacies spread out on the table religiously till they reached the corner of the table. This corner had the *thandai* laced with *bhaang*. Unaware, the two residents enjoyed their drink, tapping their feet to the background playing '*Jai jai Shiv Shankar...ye pyala tere naam ka piya*'. Soon they were back to the labour room a little elated and a little inebriated.

Unfortunately for them just at that time a 'rupture uterus' walked inside. She had been in labour for about 12 hours.

'Hey, go back home.' The senior of the two advised.

'Yes, go home. Today is Holi.' The junior repeated.

The poor patient pleaded. 'I am in pain. Where will I go?'

'*Arrey* go to professor's house. Such delicacies. Awesome drinks.'

'But my pain…!' The poor patient mumbled.

'Go home. It's Holi, a holiday. Be happy.' They kept on muttering.

'I will take you on my Scooty.' One of the drunk RSOs dramatically went on to kick-start her fictitious Scooty and drove around the labour room making silly hand and foot movements while the other one clapped and laughed hysterically.

Their *bhaang*-drugged minds had got stuck there.

Before it dawned upon the patients and became evident to everyone that they were in no state to carry on with the duty, the house surgeon who luckily had stayed back took them to the duty room and bolted them from outside. She then called the consultant on call.

Duties on festivals, especially Holi and Diwali were the most difficult to adjust and they saw the most complicated cases, especially because the private nursing homes generally remained shut.

This story was a warning for all of us. The wards were unusually busy. We rather utilised the lunch time in visiting our teachers and take their Holi blessings. We were all wiser by the day. We steered clear of all *thandais*, not that we were offered any. The consultants too were wiser. They kept all such temptations away from the emergency doctors.

An interesting case was waiting for us in the labour room casualty.

Until an hour back she was just another unmarried girl with severe pain during periods. There was no history of contact.

'I am not pregnant.' She categorically ruled out any pregnancy.

But over the years we had learned to trust our instincts more.

She worked in an airliner. Usually not the kind of patient one would have in the government hospitals but the dearth of any private centre open during Holi forced her to come here.

She had been to the casualty in the morning also, taken some analgesics and gone back home. But her pain refused to subside.

Despite her vehement denials we tested her for pregnancy and to her shock it was positive. And to make it more complicated she turned out to be a tubal ectopic pregnancy which was a pregnancy implanted in the tubes rather than the uterus and it had started to bleed. This required an urgent surgery.

'How can it happen?' She wailed.

Well, there was only one time-tested way, but we didn't say that!

Grudgingly, she admitted to having done 'that' and yes, she had taken pills to prevent conception. Teary-eyed and scared, she literally begged us not to tell her parents.

'My father is a heart patient!' She pleaded.

But a doctor had to do the dirty job. So away from her, we broke the news gently to her parents.

'How could she do it?' Her mother broke down. Her father held his chest with one hand, the other shaking at his wife's shoulder.

'When do you think this could have happened? Just tell me, please.' Her mother's mind was working overtime, already calculating the supposed time of the fatal accident.

'Was it rape?' The father exclaimed. 'You know I have 4–5 stents in my heart. You have given me a big shock. I need time to absorb this all.' He was almost breathless.

He recovered from the shock soon enough but the questions got a little more ferocious.

'Is she still in contact with this guy? Will he be coming here?' He asked.

We fumbled for an answer.

'What do you mean, maybe?'

'You can at least take a hint from her.'

'Can we find out if he's been forcing her?'

'Can we do a DNA test and nail him?'

There were questions fired right, left and centre. It was important for them to question, even if the answers were not coming from us. Probably they wanted to vent it out.

'Please be calm. Do not take it out on the girl.' The father stared as I spoke. 'She is bleeding and we do not want to disturb her. She was very concerned about both of you.'

Her friend was accompanying the parents and gradually it became evident that the patient was in relationship with a guy the parents didn't approve of. But, thankfully they decided to put up best behaviour in front of their daughter. They were better than another set of parents who in a similar situation demanded poison from the doctors for both themselves and their daughter.

Undercurrents were still rife and the atmosphere tense. The girl was shifted to the ward and unaware of what the other was going through, both parties tried to come to terms with the situation.

She was soon prepared for surgery. It is always amazing how even a little aberration was not tolerated by the very nature that had erred. Just one small offending vessel that was so easily caught at surgery was bleeding the life out of her. Around 2 litres of blood from her abdomen was removed. The tube had ruptured and was removed along with the bleeding vessel. Timely surgery and blood transfusion saved her life.

The surgery had got us late. I still needed to have my dinner. Sameer was on duty. I called him up.

'Hello, did you have your dinner?'

'Not yet. Couldn't get time from the wards.'

'Let's go out. We can be back within an hour. See, I brought you *gujjiyas* and *kachoris* that we cooked at home.' I offered him the goodies when we met.

Sameer gulped down the *kachoris* and murmured appreciatively. We went out to our favourite joint.

'We will have chilly chicken with *roti*.' If the waiter found the combination weird we gave a damn to him. We relished it.

'So are we meeting tonight?' Sameer asked. The orange-yellow lights were casting playful shadows on his face.

It was another matter that it was night, and we had already met! However, nights in the hospital were pregnant with possibilities.

'I shall try. Maybe when it's my turn to take rest.' I promised him. This was becoming a habit. These stolen moments were getting too precious.

I was just passing the antenatal wards when I heard her voice—sharp, shrill and full of abuses. She was fighting with another patient. My batch of medical students whom I was going to teach today evening listened to her shocked. She let out a string of unadulterated abuses in her local dialect. The boys burst out laughing. I was embarrassed.

'That woman is suffering from Caprolalia. It happens to some patients after they come out of eclampsia.' I told them.

'It's a disease not a habit most men suffer in this country.' I looked at them pointedly.

'What disease, Ma'am?' Gaurav, my student enquired curiously. Trust the boys for not listening. Not very long ago we were also like them.

'Don't worry, you don't suffer from it.' Another one quipped in. A bout of laughter followed. I couldn't help smiling.

'Will she be alright?' Gaurav asked.

'Let's hope she doesn't become a man.' I said and that caused a bout of laughter.

I met Anuj on the way back to labour room.

'Do you remember that patient, Krishna?' He asked me.

'Anuj, there are so many Krishnas.' I rebuked him.

'No, the one who has been coming to our infertility clinic for the past one year.' Anuj said.

'Okay! The one who was depressed and her husband was complaining that there was no progress in their treatment.' I recalled his wife who feared that he might remarry, too.

'Exactly. I met him while coming back from the OPD at the medical shop.'

'Alright.' I was not sure what this was leading to.

'You should have seen what he was buying!' Anuj sounded really excited. I waited.

'He was buying condoms!'

'Oh, but why? He was so desperate to have a child.' I was getting confused.

'That's what I thought, too. And when I said that to him, he replied, "You people think I am foolish? I listen to what they teach on television everyday. They say that if we don't use condoms we shall suffer from HIV. I never fail to use it".'

I started laughing. Ignorance wasn't always a bliss, it was sometimes a cause of all sufferings too.

'The poor guy was so proud of his knowledge.' Some people were so innocently, refreshingly stupid.

'Remember to give him some good advice.' I told Anuj.

'While we had taught them about fertile period, we never asked them to stop using condoms.' I grinned to myself.

Reminded us never to take things for granted!

Anuj was the only male doctor in the obstetrics and gynaecology department in our batch. He was often the butt of jokes amongst our batchmates.

'He's so sissy. I bet he sits and pees.' They all grinned unashamedly.

'That's so vulgar! Shut up you guys.' I was offended.

'He swings his leg from the front while riding his motor cycle.' Another guy chipped in.

'Oh really, I thought he rode a Scooty.' They slapped each other's back. We were such gender-driven insensitive people.

'You guys are so rude. I wish I could call you all racists.' I just could not bear their banter.

Anuj was married to a general surgeon and had picked up gynaecology deliberately. This was to ensure a decently running nursing home. But here the guys had ganged up against him. They were bent upon pulling his leg.

'I had gone to meet her in the labour ward.' Sameer was pointing towards me. 'She was sitting on a bench crouching with pain. Anuj was standing in front of her. He pulled her sweater's edges and said, "Hey dear, why don't you get yourself thoroughly investigated. You are always in pain".' They all burst out laughing at his mimicry. I couldn't hold back a smile.

'You all are so bad. You can't appreciate a caring guy.' I said.

'Come on, that's called girlish.' It was useless arguing with them. I left them at the scooter stand still poking jokes at poor Anuj.

There was a furore outside the main gate of the hospital. A man was abusing his wife, who was admitted in our wards. She was to undergo a hysterectomy a few days later. Anuj and I were strolling down for a quick cup of tea. As we came closer we realised that he was drunk.

He was about to slap his wife when Anuj came between them and grabbed his wrist.

'Security, just take him away.' I shouted at the security guards. They came rushing and pushed the man. The poor woman was cringing with shame yet folded her hands.

'Sir, please forgive him. He's otherwise a nice man. It's only when he gets drunk that he gets abusive,' she pleaded.

I marvelled at her tolerance.

We went to the tea stall which was hardly few yards from the hospital. We finished our tea and headed back to the ward. I still needed to wind up my work.

Just at the verge of entering the main gate, we were intercepted by the man again. There was a strong stench of liquor coming from him. I covered my nose.

He spoke deliriously, 'You think you are very smart?' His hands curled around Anuj's collar. Anuj shrugged his hands off. But the man came near again.

'I was talking to my wife. What's your problem?' He hissed.

'You are not allowed to abuse any woman. You cannot hit her even if she is your wife.' Anuj tried to reason out with him.

He was too drunk to care. Before Anuj could react, the drunken man's fist had landed on his face in a punch. Anuj was taken aback. He was red with rage. Before I could call the security, Anuj had taken off his shirt and was blowing fists on the man. Being drunk, the man didn't have much control and collapsed. By that time his wife came running and even the security guard was called.

The wife started crying, '*Maaf kar do sa'ab*.' She kept on asking for forgiveness. 'Please don't call the police.'

'It's okay. Don't worry. Send him home.' Anuj told her.

I was surprised at his display of generosity. The poor woman dragged her husband away.

'You were very brave there, Anuj.' I couldn't help gushing over him.

He flexed his muscles. 'I was enjoying there.' He grinned. Men and their strange fascinations!

I wished all the guys who were till the other day poking fun at Anuj could have witnessed this.

He put his shirt back on. The gynaecology department had found its hero. I smiled broadly.

But the story was not yet over.

A few days later Anuj found the volatile husband waiting for him at the hospital entrance once again. But this time he immediately fell down at his feet. He couldn't stop apologising over and over again. Gone was the abusive man. In his place stood a remorseful one.

'I was drunk, Sir. I am feeling so ashamed of myself.' He kept his eyes lowered. 'Please hit me. You take care of my wife and my daughter. And see how I treated you.' He was wallowing in reproach.

'That is our duty to our patients. It doesn't change with your behaviour.' Anuj reassured him.

Needless to say all was forgiven. The man remained in touch with Anuj for many years thereafter.

A couple of years later he suffered from appendicitis but refused to get operated by any surgeon other than Anuj. It was after much persuasion that he got admitted in the male surgical ward but only after he extracted a promise from Anuj that he would be part of the operating team.

Whosoever said that love wins all, had not ever suffered from a fit of anger and then a bout of guilt.

I was surprised to see Dr Bali waiting for me in the ward.

'Can you write this paper for me? It shall be published in a journal. Your name would also be there,' she said.

I was excited.

Just at that time the professor walked inside. Dr Bali handed me over the papers and left.

'Can we take the rounds?' The professor asked me pointedly.

As I walked with her she murmured, 'If you are so interested in publishing a paper, you can easily present mine.' With that she disappeared into her room leaving me bewildered.

'I think you should refrain from doing Dr Bali's paper. What is the sense of antagonising the professor?' Kavya advised me when I narrated the whole incidence to her.

I understood what she meant.

I apologised and put up some lame excuse to Dr Bali for my inability in working on her paper. She accepted calmly but my mood was spoiled.

I was on my way for lunch and thought of paying Sameer a surprise visit. That would lift my mood too. Lately I was springing lot of surprises on him, I admitted humorously.

Sameer looked up and saw me entering the ward. I quietly moved to the doctors' room and waited while he finished doing a lumber puncture.

'So, what brings you to our poor ward?' Sameer asked teasingly.

I felt a little awkward and wished I hadn't come at all. I waited for him to finish.

'Do you know about this blockbuster running in the cinema halls?' He asked as he entered the doctors' room.

I had heard about it but failed to understand the context. But before I could ask him to elaborate we were interrupted.

'Doctor *sa'ab,* his fever is not coming down.' An attendant entered with his son in his arms.

Sameer got down to explaining his reports. The little boy was suffering from polio.

'Would you come to see the movie with me?' Sameer wouldn't be asking the father! I jerked back. The man had already left with his son. We were now alone in the cabin.

Did he really mean that? And would I really?

'Don't tell me you are scared to go.' He said.

That got me. 'I am never scared.' I answered confidently. Nobody dared me. Seriously, just him and me? Nobody else! I couldn't control a wave of excitement.

However, I was not telling this to anyone, not even to Kavya. So many times I felt like discussing this barrage of changing emotions I was going through but something held me back. It was too personal and I hesitated. I needed to have a grip on things myself before I talked to anyone. Things were moving too fast, beyond my comprehension these days. Gone was the simple, non-complicated friendship Sameer and I always had.

This was heady and complex. Every morning I got up thinking I would go back to being friends but here I was, getting drawn to him like a magnet!

'Don't run away.' Sameer's teasing voice taunted my receding back. I turned and threw him a dirty look. He laughed again and I fastened my steps.

I saw her entering the labour room a little hesitant. She looked around 35 years of age. Most of our patients were in their early twenties. This one was accompanied by her husband and another couple who I learnt were her husband's younger brother and his wife.

'We have an ultrasound that says it's placenta previa, meaning an abnormal position of the placenta in the lower segment of the uterus.' I noticed some blood too on her clothes. She must have bled.

The placenta was merely dipping into the lower segment of the uterus which meant it was still possible to do a pelvic examination.

As I checked I could feel the cervix nicely dilated to around 3 cm. The soft edge of the placenta could easily be felt at the margin through the membranes. If I ruptured the membranes the head would compress the placental bed and stop bleeding. This being her third pregnancy, she stood a very good chance of pulling it through successfully. I was optimistic. It was very much an accepted management and every placenta previa didn't need a surgery.

But I still needed to inform the consultant on call.

Other than asking for blood to be arranged, my consultant was satisfied with the way the patient was being managed.

The patient already had two girls and it was the longing for a boy that had brought her here.

'*Bhaiyya-Bhabhi* were never very keen. I was the one who kept pushing them.' Admitted the brother-in-law.

The patient progressed very fast. Soon she was ready for delivery. She had already been given one unit of blood transfusion and delivered a baby boy. The family was over the moon.

But it was not yet over for them. Her placenta surprised everyone. It hid around a fistful of clot. And soon she started bleeding profusely.

There were small tears which were oozing that were stitched. She still kept losing blood. Post-partum haemorrhage, a known entity that threatens the life of a woman, cast a dark shadow over her. The very mechanism that prevented excessive loss of blood after delivery, went overboard and consumed the clotting factors, causing DIC and more bleeding. From administering blood products to fluids, from medicines to prayers, we tried all. But our every defence ended just a notch below the offence that was mounting inside her body.

As a desperate measure, we decided to shift her for surgery to remove the offending structure—her uterus. She was conscious and held her husband's hands but didn't say anything.

Before she could be shifted, before even the consultant on call could arrive she went downhill and collapsed. She never recovered from the onslaught. Her husband and her family turned to stone as she lay, covered in white, with a thick veil of silence surrounding her.

I stood feeling guilty as hell. If only we had done it differently, maybe we could have saved her.

'It is all my fault. You tried your best.' A voice said, startling me.

It was her brother-in-law, along with her husband who stood behind with folded hands.

'She was happy with our two daughters. It's actually my fault.' Her husband raised his anguished eyes.

I had seen people creating a ruckus in hospitals in grief, but here he was, thanking me, even as his world turned upside down. His humility touched me more than words can ever define and, strangely, left me feeling worse.

The formalities were completed, they were gone leaving me behind clutching a bundle of case notes in my hands. I would need to prepare a death summary again.

However it was the vacant bed that stared at me. I could still feel her there looking at me.

'My daughters are waiting for me at home.' I closed my ears.

'A caesarean was perfectly justified in placenta previa.' She prodded through my closed ears.

'I came walking to your labour room just a couple of hours back.'

If only I could run away from here.

The first half of the night was Anuj's turn to rest. I couldn't let him go. A strange fear engulfed me—very unbecoming of a doctor who had seen death at close quarters. Yet I gripped his hands. I knew I was straining him but the mere thought of being alone in the labour room terrified me.

Anuj had been a medical officer in a rural block previously. His jobs implied almost everything even post-mortem at times. He was thick-skinned, yet he understood and didn't ridicule me.

'I shall sleep on the bench inside the labour room.' Appearances were so deceptive and it was adversities that showed your true character. Once again Anuj won my respect.

Sometimes we got official reasons to move patients out of the labour room. The patients with heart diseases and jaundice were the ones that were not kept in the labour room but in the medical ward. And they generally delivered there. It meant that our responsibility was limited to the period of labour. Delivering on a bed in the medical ward was actually cumbersome but it still meant lesser responsibility. The residents from different specialities often sparred over patients.

'The patient is in labour. Why should we keep them?' Cribbed the medicine RMO (Resident Medical Officer).

'She is primarily a heart disease patient. We just need to deliver.' We answered. 'We can't keep calling you.' Not that they were very prompt in such situations either.

A consensus was reached. Till 28 weeks or roughly seven months of pregnancy the patient would be kept in the medical ward but later, unless she needed some intensive medical management, she would be in the gynaecology wards. Both departments had to work together as joint units in giving her care.

Nobody wanted to keep high-risk patients in their wards. Every department aimed to have a low mortality figure even if it meant shifting the patient as early as possible. If we didn't exactly enjoy going to other departments, the same could not be said about them as I was soon to discover.

Dr Mohan from the surgical ward stood waving a paper in his hands in our emergency. He was the surgery RSO, a third-year PG. Another medical officer accompanied him.

'There was a call for this patient.' He was standing in the doorway and appeared a little restless.

'Yeah, she has been having severe pain in her abdomen.' I said.

It was a little peculiar for him to come all the way especially with a medical officer. The calls were generally attended by the juniors. Yet, who was I to complain? The obstetrics and gynaecology department always had a dearth of handsome male residents.

'Can you take me around, err...to the patient?' Again a strange request! Why should he need an escort? But I couldn't come up with any reason to excuse myself.

Dr Mohan was my senior from MBBS days and although we knew each other by names we had hardly ever interacted.

I led him to the ward. On the way both the men kept talking to me on a wide range of topics that ranged from my parents to my siblings to my hobbies. I was piqued by their interest but couldn't help laughing at their funny rejoinders either.

The patient was seen and soon we were back. They thanked me courteously and left. I was puzzled. There was something that I couldn't put my finger onto.

It became clear soon.

'Your father has sent a marriage proposal for Mohan.' Dr Ranjan teased me while Sameer laughed.

There, that made sense! Mohan belonged to a medical background and with a flourishing nursing home, was an eligible bachelor. Sometime back I had noticed Dr Varma pointing Mohan's mother towards me in a departmental meeting. His mother was a practicing gynaecologist and Dr Varma was a pathetic matchmaker.

My father knew the medical officer who had come along with Mohan and they were all probably suffering from an acute attack of matchmaking.

I was more embarrassed than angry. I just didn't like being a butt of jokes. How could my father do this to me?

I took it out all on the poor man.

'You should have asked me first.' I told my father.

'But what have I done?' He replied, clueless.

'I told you that I don't want to get married, and definitely not to a doctor!' I was livid.

'But, what's wrong with him?' Dad asked.

'He went around telling the whole world about this proposal.' I shuddered at the embarrassment it caused me.

I don't know what hurt more, the proposal or the fact that the world knew about it. Obviously, my father didn't like to see me upset. The news got to Mohan and eventually back to me.

'I was not interested in marrying her. It was just a proposal, an idea flouted by our parents and well wishers. I had told only my friend. I don't know how everyone got to know about it.' He told everyone defensively.

That friend happened to be an anaesthetist who was a mutual friend to many of us. Anaesthetists and their penchant for gossips!

In our college with its ancient buildings there were no secrets. A story breathed in every corner. It gave me more reasons to be discreet when I met Sameer. But then there were times when you were ready to throw caution to the winds. And I was doing just that, planning my Sunday date with him.

Finally, it was Sunday. I was supposed to finish my rounds first and then go to the much-anticipated movie.

She was just about seven months pregnant yet her abdomen was so bloated because of her twin gestation that she looked as if she was about to burst. With so much discomfort in walking, her efforts became almost palpable. And, on top of that, she was breathless. Her babies were surrounded by excessive fluid and that worsened things.

'Madam, please relieve me now. I can't carry further.' She had said this umpteen times.

The excessive fluid surrounding the babies had to be drained. Normally the news of twin pregnancy was greeted with lots of intrigue and excitement but they generally followed a tumultuous course.

'Once the fluid has come out, you will feel much better.' I assured her.

I shifted her into the labour room and inserted a long needle through her abdomen and soon clear fluid started draining. We were almost half way through our set target when she started feeling more breathless. Worried, I tried to feel her pulse. There was none. Not even the other hand. I tried to measure her BP. That too couldn't be measured. Why the hell was she in shock?

I shouted for help. Fortunately, it was morning and I could gather assistance. The needle was taken out and the fluid stopped from draining further. Thankfully, the patient was conscious. After some injections, some fast fluids and some beats that my heart missed, soon the precious pulse reappeared and along with it came the blood pressure. My own blood pressure that had shot high started a gradual descent.

And somewhere between all this I had forgotten all about Sameer.

I had almost missed my movie date. I rushed outside.

Sameer was waiting for me, a little restless.

'Look at the watch!' He said.

I shrugged.

He understood where our priorities lay. A movie could be missed but life never gave you another chance. It was a feeling that drove him too, an almost primal instinct of saving another human being.

By the time we reached, we had missed the first 15 minutes of the movie but we were least bothered.

However, halfway through the movie, I had never been more awkward. The adjacent seats brought us too close and the darkness surrounding us added to the intimacy. The movie was interesting but then somehow we were not there. I was too conscious not only of Sameer, but of every other person around. Suddenly, I felt a warm sensation on my arms. Sameer's arm casually draped around my shoulder was making circles on my bare arm. I brushed it away before it went down further.

I turned my head towards him about to say something and found his face too near. He smelled of fresh cologne and I inhaled the fragrance deeply. His breath fanned my cheeks and I could see his mouth dropping towards mine. I panicked.

'Sameer, can we go out?' I asked him hesitantly. I didn't want to look gauche or foolish.

To my relief he agreed.

'Let's go to the juice centre,' Sameer proposed. I nodded. I was guilty of spoiling our date.

We were surprised to find Dr Ranjan in the juice centre but I was relieved to have company.

'I can see a new watch there.' Dr Ranjan observed. Indeed it was and I was thankful someone noticed. Sameer never did!

We left the juice centre on Sameer's scooter. Suddenly a bicycle swerved dangerously in front of his scooter.

'What the hell!' Sameer exclaimed. The scooter turned dangerously and skidded. Sameer lost his balance and both of us landed on the road with a thud.

It took me a few minutes to gather my senses. I rose shrugging off the dust from my clothes.

Unfortunately, Sameer couldn't get up so easily. He was in a lot of pain.

'Are you hurt?' Dr Ranjan was also leaning over Sameer. His forearm had swollen and angry bruises ran over his limbs.

We immediately took him to the casualty unit. An X-ray confirmed a fracture of the humerus. He had no choice but to get a plaster. If I was feeling guilty earlier, I felt worse now. This was not the way my first date should have ended.

It was getting late and I checked my watch for the time. I was appalled. My empty wrist stared back at me.

My new watch! Probably when I was thrown on the road, my watch too had followed. But in all the confusion I had failed to notice it on the roads, or felt its absence on my wrist.

'Can we go back and check it?' Dr Ranjan nodded. It was a futile exercise as it was nowhere to be seen. My new watch was gone.

Next day, Dr Ranjan called me up.

'What have you done to Sameer? Even when he was knocked out he kept on gushing about you. "She's such a sweet girl," he kept on repeating.' Dr Ranjan was observing me closely while his eyes crinkled with a teasing smile.

A floodgate of emotions burst through me and I blushed. I was as confused as embarrassed. Somehow

Sameer made me a little guilty in front of my friends. They trusted me so much and here I was hiding things from them.

Sameer was back to his old ward but with a broken forearm and a plaster, that was on the way to become a masterpiece. It was inevitable with so many autographs splayed all over by his constant flow of well-wishers and friends. Fortunately, the fracture was not in the right forearm so he could continue to carry on with his work.

But it meant he couldn't drive. It was my Scooty that stepped in and it took us around.

We spent the afternoons together. We often went to 'Mandre ki Mata', a temple situated on a hill just near the hospital, but never actually inside. A small, narrow path led uphill to an isolated spot, a grove which was an idyllic haven for those in search of some privacy.

Strangely, I was no longer plagued by what others said or felt. I loved being in his company and I didn't care about what anyone else said. People did get an inkling that something was going on. But they couldn't tell for sure, whether it was me or Kavya that Sameer was going around with. We all had been together for so long that some confusion was bound to happen.

The long list of caesareans that continued all through the night tired us. Not every patient that walked inside the labour room, any time of the day or night was welcomed. Sometimes, we groaned too and took it out on them. The prospect of doing a surgery in the middle of night didn't exactly fill anyone with delight. The biological diurnal clock forcing the body to sleep was pitched against the patients forcing us to be awake. And so it jarred more when the anaesthetist whom we were compelled to wake up for our midnight surgical adventures grumbled.

'What's the problem with you girls? Why is every patient of yours in foetal distress?'

'But it was an emergency.'

'You girls cook up an emergency just to do a surgery or maybe you want to finish off the case in your own time.' This was their never-ending grievance.

'The baby's heart rate was dropping to 80!'

'But the fluid was clear, no meconium.' They refused to believe us. And then they would do their utmost to postpone the case. From her blood reports to her stomach being full, to not fasting, they tried their best.

'Anaesthetists and gynaecologists are like husband and wife.' I had dropped a bombshell. This anaesthetist, a Casanova, was suddenly all ears.

'I am interested to know more.' He looked at me obliquely.

'Neither can they live with each other nor without each other.' I laughed. He smiled, clearly not liking the analogy.

Three caesareans later, that night they left the fourth one lying outside. She was placenta previa and bleeding.

Yet, my erstwhile colleague felt that it was not enough to warrant an emergency.

'Her vitals are stable. There is no active bleeding.' They decided and left.

The gynaecology residents were at the receiving end from one and all, especially from our own consultants. On the contrary nobody could ever dare complain to the anaesthesia consultants about their residents. They always sprang to their defence. Unfairness sucks and so did this one.

The morning team had arrived to take over. They looked at us suspiciously and we bristled. The 'pending case' was not our doing. Leaving them at the operation theatre to take the patient inside I finished my rounds and went to the labour room.

Suddenly there was a loud noise from the corner of the labour room. It was the sound of steel vessels striking against each other. Curious, I reached there. I was almost sure that it was the cat again when I noticed that a delivered patient was repeatedly hitting a large steel bowl kept near her feet on the corner of the labour table. It was full of water.

Why should the ward *bai* keep that bowl there and why should the patient hit at it repeatedly, I had no clue. But as I approached her, I realised that the patient was having a seizure. Oh god, not another case of eclampsia! But that's what it was precisely. She was started on anticonvulsants and shifted to the eclampsia room. Fortunately, the baby had been delivered before she had thrown a fit.

The eclampsia room was getting crowded and this was going to continue. If only people rose above prejudices, shed off some bias and started going to hospitals, well in time for their checkups!

Each passing day was making us more and more proficient. By now we had assisted in almost all kinds of surgeries and could independently do most of the basic ones like hysterectomy (uterus removal), caesarean and MTP (medical termination of pregnancy). It was MTP that we got to do in plenty.

In the early months of pregnancy, the uterus was evacuated of its contents, which we called POCs, by suction. The house surgeons had an unusual duty. When the suction jar got full, they had to sieve it. The idea was to check the contents for any abnormal products. It was definitely not something we looked forward to and often tried to engage the ward *bai* into doing it.

It was one such suction that sprang a surprise.

'Hey look, what's this?' I shouted excitedly at Kavya.

'It's an intact foetus in a clear unruptured sac!' Kavya said, equally astonished.

The six-week-old foetus lay glistening in a clear replication of the text book pictures and filled us with awe.

'Now I realise why our seniors are wary of doing MTP.' I looked at our amazing discovery.

For some unexplained reason we never threw it away. We preserved it in a small glass vial and kept it in our cupboard. And, it stayed inside even when we handed over the cupboard to our juniors at the end of our term.

'MTP is going to be your bread and butter.' We were told.

And the number of women thronging the family planning units made sure we became smart and familiar with the procedure.

A young girl stood silently in a corner. She would be around eighteen years of age and had come for an abortion. Her mother was admitted in the female medical ward in our hospital for a long time. It was strange how everyone was familiar with her and majority of these were our own residents in the medical and surgical wards.

The duty room in the female medical ward was in a secluded corner on the top floor. It was always shrouded with rumours and the story surrounding this girl was equally scandalous.

'Don't you think it's strange that these guys are calling up almost everybody in our department for her?' Kavya whispered to me.

I nodded. I had received a call in the morning from a colleague who knew I was posted in the family planning OT.

'Please take care of her. Her family is known to me.' I was told.

And as we took her inside the theatre, our senior medical officer came in.

'My relative called me up for her.'

Her relative worked in the surgery department. He was a popular resident. Most of the staff competed with each other to please him. The boys would often make snide remarks about him.

But, lately he was found more often in the middle of controversies, some of them serious enough to find their way into newspapers. There was one about a female patient who had levelled serious allegations against him. It not only brought a bad name to his family but tarnished the reputation of our hospital as well. I had always been wary of him.

But, something was definitely fishy today. I didn't get much time to brood over it as I soon got busy with another patient. I was struggling to dilate the cervix.

'It is so tightly closed. How will I empty the uterus if I cannot enter it?' I spoke to the nurse assisting me. Despite all my efforts it refused to dilate. I looked around helplessly. Dr Varma was posted in the OT.

'Any problem?' She asked me. I was feeling a little awkward after that disastrous goof-up with Mohan. I had failed her attempts at matchmaking.

But she was always that bold surgeon who was famously called Daku Varma—derived from the way her name, Dr Kumud Varma, was written in Hindi.

'I am unable to dilate the cervix.' I told her.

Dr Varma took charge. She put the dilator inside with force. It went straight inside.

'Ma'am, the length is just 8 cm. Don't you think it's going a little beyond?' I was worried.

'You must learn not be scared in surgery.' She advised me.

'Here goes the next dilator. Now the cervix is nicely open. I will now put the forceps inside and start bringing out the POCs (products of conception). Look here.'

She boldly pulled out yellowish-coloured tissue. But strangely it didn't look like POCs. It was more like omentum!

'Err, this looks like omentum,' she admitted.

Omentum was the tissue guarding the gut and usually the first thing to be caught by a forceps in the event of a perforation of the uterus.

'Call the professor,' she said.

The professor walked inside and was briefed about the case. Immediately she put a laparoscope inside the abdomen and confirmed the wrong path that our instruments had taken inside. There was a rent, which we called a perforation on the top of the uterus.

'If you are a gynaecologist and have never done a perforation in the uterus, it means either you are not a gynaecologist or you have never done an MTP.' The professor's reasoning seemed to have worked more on Dr Varma who appeared much quieter.

'It's alright to do a complication. But it's more important to recognise one,' the professor assured.

Agreed, a perforation should never go home unrecognised. But, why was the professor looking at me? I turned to look at Dr Varma, imploring her to own up but she was not looking at me.

It sounded churlish to say that it wasn't me responsible for the complication. My inability to speak out frustrated me just as much as her intentional silence.

The patient had to undergo a surgery but at least we had averted a nightmare by timely stitching the rent.

Now well into the second month of my family planning posting some of Dr Varma's confidence had rubbed over me. The hospital politics were too hot those days, and in all the debates going on in the theatre, I simply didn't measure the size of the uterus. I was now smart enough to measure it with any instrument. However, this was a lactating woman with a very thin uterine wall that I missed and ended up doing a perforation. I rushed to call the consultant from the main OT. It was stitched.

But as my luck would have it, the very next day I repeated the mistake. This time the instrument I used to hold the cervix to pull it forward slipped, just at the time when I was dilating it. The result was that my dilator went straight inside and then out of the uterus inside the abdomen, barely missing the urinary bladder.

I once again rushed to the main OT.

'Not again!' Cried the consultant.

The patient was opened and stitched. She was discharged in a few days but it shook my confidence badly. For days I was absorbed in guilt. Even if not intentional, a patient had been inconvenienced, forced to overstay in the hospital. It clawed at me.

Raj was waiting for me.

'I am getting married!'

He was the first among the boys of my batch to do so. It filled me with excitement still I looked at him thoughtfully.

'Are you really sure about this?'

His fiancée was doing her post-graduation in gynaecology from Indore.

'Why do all guys get married to gynaecologists?' I wondered.

I never knew Parul had a soft corner for Raj. It were the days following his engagement that gave her away. But then that's what infatuations are, a sweet ache that teases you and eventually dies a slow but sure death. Soon Parul too found the 'love' of her life.

Raj's marriage brought all our batchmates together. It also gave Sameer and me plenty of time to be together. In all the festivities, none of us noticed the strain that occasionally flashed on Raj's face. His marriage had given all of us memories of a lifetime and a break from our predictable and gruelling routine.

Barely a few had months passed when I met a much-distraught Raj again.

'Shreya has left for Indore.' He sounded low. She could barely manage leaves and neither could he. The pressure of a long-distance relationship was clearly evident on his face.

'Soon it will be Diwali. I am sure she will be back.' He nodded and left.

His wife was a simple girl. Studies had never left her with much time to train in household chores.

And it didn't help when her shortcomings started getting pointed out by Raj's family.

'I am trying to adjust. But at every step there is a roadblock in the name of tradition and rituals.' She sobbed once in front of me.

Raj's parents too were having problems adjusting to a daughter-in-law who was perennially absent and was contrary to the image of a stereotyped housewife they had foolishly expected.

A marriage needed a strong foundation to build upon. Their erratic schedules hardly left them with any time to invest in their relationship. I kept my fingers crossed. They would find their way through. It was a matter of just two more years.

Meanwhile, marriage was becoming a 'bone of contention' in the families of majority of our batchmates. Most parents felt compelled to settle down their children despite being aware of their hardships. They couldn't shrug off the social pressures. We were far from settled and none of us was financially strong yet.

Kavya too was busy fending off prospective grooms who came visiting her in the hospital often under some pretext or the other while she wanted to marry much later. Fortunately, her parents didn't pressurise her much.

It was much different for Varun though. His mother wanted him to run his own nursing home. He was pursuing a postgraduate degree in surgery and being a practical person she wanted him to marry a gynaecologist.

Varun fell in love easily, in fact many a times during our MBBS days but never serious enough and unfortunately always one sided.

'I do not want to move out and pursue surgery.' He had been most reluctant.

'Surgeons get to marry gynaecologists,' I teased him.

He looked at me thoughtfully and said, 'You will have to find me one.'

I never knew he was being serious.

'There are so many eligible girls in your department. I want to see Varun settled.' His mother came to see me one day.

Parul was my friend and the only eligible girl I could think of for him. I just flouted the idea to both of them and incredibly they both agreed. I was turning out to be a perfect matchmaker.

Their marriage once again put us in a festive gear.

Those days I reached home quite late and would often be dropped by Sameer, something that didn't go down well with my mother.

'We live in a closed society. Being a doctor doesn't mean that you are above all restrictions that society imposed on us,' my mother complained.

My parents had always trusted me. I felt a little guilty. But parental pressure and their objection was one thing we were getting adept at. Our work made us thick-skinned and headstrong.

As always her eyes made me tongue-tied!

There was something about her that unnerved me. I could never understand her.

And neither could I comprehend her signals today. Her deft finger working their way through cutting and suturing were now earnestly asking for something.

Her eyes as they stared at me from between her mask and the cap looked irritated. Confusion marred my eyes as I looked back at her.

'Where is your attention?' She seemed to be warning me.

She was pointing with her right index finger towards the uterus that was slowly getting removed. Suddenly, I felt a movement. My senior, the first assistant had brought the suction there.

She wanted the field to be cleared by suction! I was not yet familiar with her techniques and it was getting frustrating, following her silent instructions.

I had been reluctant to scrub along with her.

'There is no one else,' my senior entreated. 'You are not a coward to run away from the battle.' She reproached me. This was no ordinary battle.

I was concentrating hard on keeping the operating field clear. I held on to the retractors and in between used the sponges to mop out the blood.

'You have to understand her sign language.' Our seniors often told us. What was wrong in being a little vocal?

She was pointing again. This time she brought her index finger towards her thumb and snapped the two fingers in rapid, repetitive movements.

She wanted to close something. Wow, I got that!

She wanted an artery forceps to hold an oozer spoiling the field. That was close. But the battle was only half won.

From asking for forceps, to suction, mops, or a pair of scissors, there was always a hand movement, a sign to convey that. It wasn't just a surgery but a battle of wits. I wished I had played more puzzle games.

And then there was always a right way to hand over the instrument.

'Our professor used to hit our fingers with the handle of her instrument,' recounted a friend doing her post-graduation from another institute. 'And if you passed on the wrong one, she threw them on the floor in anger.' I was thankful we didn't have to face such antics.

But above all it was a treat watching her operating. She was an accomplished surgeon and had an edge over the rest.

She taught us an important lesson, 'Never lose your calm especially when there is a complication. And if you cannot deal with the complications, you haven't learnt surgery well enough.'

We were all at different levels in the learning curve and it was comforting to have someone around to pull you out when you sent an SOS message.

Sometimes we strayed beyond our fields. Our biggest enemies were the errant bowel and urinary bladder that came in our way. And we sometimes ended up injuring them. These were the times when we had to call the surgeon.

There were very few hunks in our college and he was one of them. Most of the girls had drooled over him during our MBBS days. The thickly adherent bowel and the subsequent bowel injury during a surgery had brought him to our operation theatre today. We had reasons to be happy when Anurag, now a final-year post-graduate arrived instead of his boss and did the repair.

The patient was shifted into the recovery ward and I went to check her postoperatively.

'Open your eyes!' I shook her.

'You should never wake up a person while sleeping.' I heard a deep voice from behind.

I didn't know Anurag had followed me to see the patient. I suddenly felt nervous.

'Why?' I asked, surprised.

'You will start coming in their dreams,' he said in a smooth tone.

'Oh, come on. That's not true.' I said.

'When I am sleeping, wake me up once. You will start coming in my dreams,' he said, dramatically.

He was obviously an accomplished flirt. I couldn't help sharing this with my friends later.

'Oh mere khwabon mein tum!' Sameer sang crudely.

'Oh dear, now I know why I dream so much.' Our anaesthetist friend said.

'Also, why do you wake up only female patients?' Raj teased him.

Anurag was renamed 'Wake me up, before you go go' and that became a hit! I just couldn't help laughing whenever I passed by him.

The operation theatres taught more than mere surgeries.

Like the one time when I was assisting Dr Batra in a surgery. I always felt more at ease with her. She had an aura around her, even when she was operating.

The main job of the assistant was to make things easier for the surgeon. I was trying hard to do it, with both my hands.

'There are two places when you should never cross your hands.' She told me. 'One is during surgery. If you cross your hands, you strain more and block the view too.' She continued. I hastily corrected my hands and things definitely started looking better.

'So, now you realise why you were getting stuck?' She smiled. 'Can you now guess the other?'

I tried hard but gave up.

'It's driving! You can never do that with your hands crossed!'

That was a golden lesson. I tried driving my Scooty that day with crossed hands and laughed at myself. Years later when I learned driving a car I would often cross my hands on the steering wheel, remember Dr Batra and give up, with a smile on my face.

It was not an exaggeration but the operation theatre and the labour room were our true '*karmabhoomi*', our action-packed battlefield.

And they taught us so much more, beyond surgeries.

In all my medical college days if there was one subject that made me shudder, it was forensic medicine or jurisprudence. It neither appealed to me nor did I ever enjoy it. I dreaded both the books and the practicals, equally. The visuals disturbed me. At night I would cover the horrific images of drowning and electrocution, amongst many more gruesome ones that stared at me from my textbooks. It filled me with a sense of death, an unpleasant feeling.

The post-mortems that were mandatory filled me with disgust, remorse and many unnamed, mixed feelings. Probably, I suffered from necrophobia, the fear of the dead. That disgusting stench surrounding the dead bodies, most of them decomposed beyond recognition, made me nauseous. All I wanted to do was shut my eyes and run away. But forget that, we were not allowed to even cover our noses. It was a mark of disrespect. Though I meant no offence to those who took up the subject, rather I found them very brave, I promised myself this was one place that would never find me, at least not in this life.

This was in sharp contrast to my anatomy days. The first-year MBBS spent in the dissection hall with the cadavers were still the most memorable days of medical college. But forensics was a different ball game. Probably it was a reminder of the gruesome death some people suffered or maybe it was a deep aversion to the unnatural manner of death rather than the dead itself.

It was just not my day, when I got a call from my consultant.

'Two bodies have been found in the forests of Morena. They are being brought to the mortuary in Gwalior. When they call, you must be present there,' she told me.

'Ma'am, please, I can't be there.' I literally begged. My stomach was clenching in revulsion.

'Listen, this is a sensational murder case. There will be a lot of press coverage too.'

'But...'

'How can we refuse?'

I was about to ask her to come herself but words failed me. That would sound so unprofessional. Moreover, a junior could never command a senior. The medical ethos never worked that way.

An hour later, my colleague Bani and I were standing in the post-mortem room surrounded by the familiar sense of nausea. This time I was not a student there. I covered my nose.

'Do you think we are stupid or lesser people who stand here with our nose uncovered and our eyes open?' The forensic medicine professor said sarcastically to the police officer who had his nose covered too.

I removed my hand. The pointer was not lost.

There were two women. The bodies were thrown into the jungle around a day back and had been devoured by animals before being noticed by some passerby.

They looked as sordid as the tale of misery surrounding their lives.

One woman's face looked ghastly with fragments of muscle, bones and deep, bony eye sockets. Animals had eaten major parts of her limbs. As per news she had been very beautiful and the suspected accused was said to be obsessed with her. Could love bring upon you such a savage end?

There wasn't much scope for a detailed post-mortem as most of her body had been devoured by the animals. Her muscles were jutting out and her half-eaten bones lay exposed and projected from her limbs.

How painful would it be for her loved ones to look at her in this state! I shuddered. She had been kidnapped and then strangulated on the way from Delhi to Agra and later thrown in the jungles.

The other girl had been pregnant. She was still wearing the orange t-shirt and jeans that she must have been wearing when she left her house. It somehow made things more poignant.

The technician removed her clothes. He made a bold incision on her body in a sweeping, practiced stroke. The forensic medicine professor stood guiding and observing each step as the technician went on exposing the inside story to his scrutinising eyes. He was opening every cavity, collecting the visceral contents. The stomach contents told when and what she last had for dinner. Hidden in these organs breathed her story, her suffering, recreating that dreadful finale. The forensic department was delving deep, focussed on uncovering every secret buried inside her.

Her jeans lay torn over her thighs, which tapered off to two long, slender bones with fragments of muscles pointing towards what might have once been beautiful legs. They might have danced, they might have enticed and they might have provoked the beast who trapped and killed her and then threw her in the jungle to be feasted upon by the animals. Plundered by both human and the wild! Did anyone deserve such a cruel fate? And what about the fate that awaited her parents and those who loved her? A once warm, beautiful face, torn by the hungry barbarians both in the city and the jungle now reduced to a skeleton staring from the deep, bony sockets.

The technician parted her bony legs and I shivered. It was neither the warm hands of a lover nor the cold hands of a clinician, not even the cruel hands of a barbarian who touched her, but the curious, discerning eyes of a forensic expert and his technician. How easily death stripped off all the gloss that life accumulated over the years.

He exposed the perineum and vagina of the girl. The forensic medicine specialist looked at us. We looked at all that we try to hide in life. Vaginal samples and swab were taken.

A detailed post-mortem was similarly carried on the other girl as well.

I stood disgusted.

Yet, I admired the resilience of the forensic department. Just a few days here and I would grow disenchanted with life. But he stood amidst the smell of death and gore, with uncovered nose and inquisitive eyes!

I respected him, seriously, but my part was over. I didn't want to prolong my stay.

'Sir, can we go? Our labour room is packed.' I didn't in the least bit feel guilty. It was an excuse that was very handy at the moment.

He nodded. Even if he was aware that we wanted to escape he didn't give any indication. He didn't even look at us.

We heaved a sigh of relief to be back to our own territory. It was not just about the place but the tale that hung over the post-mortem room that made one revulse.

Next day, I stared at the vibrant faces of the girls as they swarmed all over the television and national dailies. They had lively eyes and beautiful smiles, so unlike the skeletonised forms that I had seen. The sensational case was called the 'triple-murder case'.

The first girl was a diet counsellor. A counsellor with the municipal corporation in Delhi was obsessed with her but she had always spurned his advances. He suspected that she was involved with the owner of the health chain that she worked for. The obsessed lover had staged her abduction. He hired professional killers who were to kidnap her for a ransom. They were to implicate the owner of the health chain with her kidnapping. And he would then pay the ransom and hopefully win her affection by acting as her saviour. The owner of the health chain was also kidnapped and murdered at a different place. But the plan took a dangerous turn when fed up with the girl's constant rebuffs, he got her murdered too. The other girl in the orange t-shirt was an employee of the health chain and was unfortunately accompanying her on the fatal day.

'There is a press conference in the forensic department. You have to attend it.' Our consultant informed us the next day.

'Oh! What are we going to say if they ask us to comment about rape?' I asked.

'Just say, "the bodies were badly decomposed. Any comment about rape can be made only after reports of chemical analysis".'

We sat on a round table in the department of forensic medicine facing the camera and the press. At any other time I would have felt important and excited. But, at that moment, I felt subdued.

The visual flashes of the victims had made it much more tragic. Till the other day they were just bodies. Today, they had an identity, a story and there were 'real' people who loved them and were grieving for them.

'So, can you tell us if there was any sexual interference with the women?' One reporter asked.

'Had they been raped?'

What had been committed was beyond rape, so heinous!

The forensic medicine professor looked at Bani and me.

Taking the cue, we stuttered the already prepared answer. The professor smiled. He had probably heard the rehearsed lines many times.

Our job was over. I hoped we were not called by any court. There were dangerous people involved. And this was one case we didn't want to be a part of at all.

I fervently hoped my brief interlude with the forensic department was over.

Some emergency duties started on a wrong note.

Sudha's mother-in-law was shouting at her. I called her husband.

'Your wife is still not well. Why is your mother shouting at her?' I asked him.

'My mother says she's a witch.' He bowed his head.

'What!'

'She gave birth to a monster. And on top of it she's childless.'

Sudha had been in the antenatal ward for a couple of months but then barely into the seventh month of gestation she went into active labour. With multiple miscarriages, her pregnancy was fret with complications. We still had high hopes for her but it lay shrivelled as we stared at a malformed, grotesque baby of about 1 kg. She developed infection as well and started suffering from high-grade fever.

I was still brooding when Sameer found me.

'Let's go to the library,' he offered.

The library in the paediatric department was on the second floor. It was a little lonely but then I just wanted to be out of the gynaecology ward for a while. I agreed.

'But isn't that closed at this time?' I asked Sameer.

'You are talking to the senior demonstrator of the department.' Sameer flaunted the keys in his hand.

'I am impressed.' I said with a smirk.

We went inside the library. Sameer closed the door and leaned against it. I had never been alone with him like this and felt a tinge of excitement creeping in.

'Don't you think people will wonder who's inside the library?' I wanted to break the tension that suddenly enveloped us.

'How would anybody know? Don't worry, nobody comes here at this time.' Sameer sounded confident.

He came to sit close to me and casually slung his arm around me.

'Hey!' I raised my hands to push him away but he held them. I could feel his warm breath. Till now all he had touched were at the little veins in my hand. This was serious!

My heartbeat quickened. I looked up to find myself staring into his eyes. Phew, they appeared fixed and dilated.

'Wait, your pupils are not reacting!' My voice sounded rushed. His thumb ran over my cheeks in a gentle caress.

'Are you going to trace the course of the facial artery on my face?' He laughed and traced the artery from my chin till it throbbed dangerously at the angle of my lips.

Hold it! Were we going to share our first kiss?

Suddenly, there was the sound of approaching footsteps and somebody drawing near. There were muffled voices and as they came closer we realised with horror it was that of Dr Ramani, the paediatric consultant on call. He must have chosen this time to see a patient in the ward.

All colour drained from my face. I silently cursed my decision to come here. Even Sameer looked a little tense. He went on to put off the light but I stopped him.

'He will see the unlatched door.' I reasoned.

The footsteps stopped in front of the door. There was a firm knock.

'Who is inside the library at this time?' Dr Ramani shouted from outside. He must have been concerned about somebody breaking in.

Sameer had no choice but to open the door. I went to sit as far as possible from him.

'Good evening, Sir.' He said.

'What are you doing here at this time, Sameer?' He stepped in to notice me sitting inside, buried in the registers.

'Sir, the gynaecology resident is working on her thesis. She wanted to check something in the library.' Sameer replied.

'At this time?' He was not impressed.

'Sir, residents don't get time during the day. She was free now and so she requested me.' Sameer replied calmly.

If he found that strange, Dr Ramani didn't say anything. Neither did he comment on anything about the door being locked from inside.

'Okay. Lock the door properly from outside when you leave.' He said and left.

I took a deep breath.

'Let's move out of here.' I told Sameer.

'But why? He has gone now.'

The mood was broken. And I was too apprehensive. Despite the keys, the library was now out of bounds for me, on any duty.

But where there is a will there is a way. We found safer alternatives.

I was the one who lived the farthest from the hospital. There were no spare rooms in the hostel for day scholars. Taking pity on me I was allotted a room on the first floor of the hospital, just next to the ward. I was allowed to use it during my duty hours to rest and have my meals as well as to freshen up. I had kept an electric stove and minimal provisions to make tea and snacks there.

It served the purpose very well. It was also a perfect place for 'us' to blossom, away from the prying eyes of the world.

Exams were a difficult time for everyone. Even the undergraduate exams! They strained the whole department, especially the postgraduates and more so the demonstrators.

'I am sick of being literally in the hospital continuously for the last couple of days.' I cribbed to Sameer.

If you were in merit it was a moment of pride, but as a PG, the first two in merit became the demonstrators.

There I was, the second demonstrator, clearly evasive and cringing at the very thought of becoming one.

Being a demonstrator imposed extra responsibilities. They were in-charge of the teaching roster, for conducting the lectures and exams of the undergraduates.

Till the responsibility part it was great but then it also meant being in close proximity with the head of the department, the professor. That is where it became worse.

Here I was, trying my very best to become invisible in front of her but there, as a demonstrator I was constantly pushed in the line of fire.

'I feel so uncomfortable.' I confessed to Kavya.

My saving grace was the first demonstrator, Payal, who suffered no such aversions. She looked after the professor's classes while I looked after Dr Bali's, our second internal. However, my presence on her side was never appreciated by our boss.

'I promise to do all the paper work. You just go inside and take her signatures.' I pushed Payal inside the HOD's chamber. Unlike others vying for her attention, I preferred to fade in the background.

'If the undergraduates don't attend classes, we are pulled up. If the teachers don't take their classes again it is our fault.' I often rued in front of Sameer. He laughed.

'Don't worry. It's the same everywhere.' He too was a demonstrator in his department.

'If the undergraduates show good knowledge then it is their exemplary learning but if they don't fare well, it is all the result of our poorly conducted classes.' I complained.

We had to make sure the postgraduates were taking the evening clinics of the medical students.

'From escorting the examiners to making arrangements for their stay, to putting up proper cases for the practicals, it's killing me now.' Sameer looked at me sympathetically as I went on and on with my complaints.

'At least you don't have to go to pick up the externals from the station at 4 am!' He exclaimed. That was true. Being a girl brought some reprieve.

'If I see the boss coming from one side, I run to the other side.' Sameer laughed. We were all still very immature not realising the importance of building a relationship with your internal examiners.

My behaviour haunted me and I could never get over the feeling that I was not close to my professor.

What I failed to appreciate as a young postgraduate was the maturity and the ability of the teachers especially your professor to look through you.

We were now unbelievably in the third year. Time was moving fast. Third year meant being directly in the line of fire! Third year also meant I would be handing over the responsibility of intern in-charge to my juniors soon. Internship, the carefree period of medical studies, was now hopelessly drowned in preparing for the pre-PG exams. Though we were always short of manpower and always needed extra pairs of hands, I could very easily let them go and study. But all this sympathy was before I was made the intern in-charge in my second year.

I had strict instructions from our teacher Dr Batra, who was the consultant in-charge of interns—no proxy, no false attendance. The obstetrics and gynaecology department was one place where the interns got no leverage. We even put them on night rolls.

The girls still managed to comply, but the boys gave me nightmares. They were never serious about their postings. And this is where it got really ugly. Some of the chronic ones, who were never seen even during their final year and always made it through their proxy attendance, were now in serious trouble.

Each of the interns was assigned a ward.

'Ask them to first get their attendance signed from their ward in-charges. Then you have to countersign it.

After I check your signature, I shall sign it and then send it to the head of the department.' Dr Batra told me.

The girls generally managed to overcome the road-blocks with minimal hiccups. Most of the boys somehow cajoled their ward in-charges into giving the pricey attendance.

Majority of the interns got their 'push and pull' from my own batchmates.

'Why do you trouble them so much for a mere attendance? And stop calling them *"beta"*.' My batchmates mocked me. Calling the interns '*beta*' was a legacy of gynaecology department, much to their amusement.

I had very strict consultants above me and they didn't let them have the easy way out. So, our signatures remained pricey.

There were some absentees who were noticed by the consultants too.

Chandan looked more like a ruffian than a doctor. His downturned moustache and the *chandan teeka* adorning his forehead gave him a foreboding look. He kept one leg on a stool and towered over me. I looked at him warily. Once upon a time, Gwalior was famous for Chambal and its bandits. Chandan looked like one of them.

'If you think I cannot manage a signature, you are wrong. I know how to have my way around here,' he threatened.

'It's not in my hands. Your absence has been noted in the registers by Dr Batra. Why don't you talk to her?' I shrugged helplessly.

'She is the one who has sent me to you.'

This was really ridiculous. Suddenly, I saw the professor coming for rounds. As I left him to take her around the wards, I had an idea.

'Why don't you ask her? She is the head of department. She can help you.'

He immediately disappeared into the professor's office. Very soon he came out, wearing a sourer expression than before.

'She said I had no business going to her directly. She countersigns only the ones that are signed by Dr Batra.' As I gave an expression that said 'I told you', he added, 'You are harassing me, Madam. I will set you right soon.' He left threatening me.

Soon I was called by the head of the department.

'Why are you sending the interns to me? If you can't handle them, you should talk to Dr Batra.'

I came back and flopped in my ward deep in thoughts. I refused to admit but I was scared of Chandan.

'You should sign his attendance tomorrow. Why invite trouble?' Kavya said. I was actually feeling a little intimidated. My decision was made.

I met Sameer later in the day and voiced my thoughts. Though he was a channel through which most interns pushed their attendance, he understood my dilemma.

'Don't worry. We will sort this out.' He assured me.

A couple of days later when I entered my ward I saw Chandan waiting for me. The moment he saw me, he fell on my feet.

'Please hit me, Madam, for I have sinned.'

My eyes rolled upwards. Had he gone mad?

'Sameer Sir told me about you. I worship him. He's been my guru since my first-year days.'

Ah, now things were falling in place.

He went on taking the names of my batchmates and how he revered them. My decision was already made a day before, even before he came singing praises of my batchmates to me. I signed his attendance sheet and sent him to Dr Batra.

My 'one' signature sent into roll a lot more. Some solutions were simple. We just needed to see them with a different perspective.

Mortality was not uncommon in our wards. But every time a patient died, something inside us snapped. A young life lost at the altar of childbirth! Were we destined to be known for 'Taj Mahal', a monument that breathes the story of a queen losing her life at the altar of her thirteenth childbirth? A staggeringly high maternal mortality rate and other gender-skewed statistics remained a blot on our national pride even so many years post independence.

Anaemia, haemorrhage, hypertension and unsafe abortion laid the tombstone in majority cases. The septic-labour room and the eclampsia room that housed these patients carried a red herring! In those days when the standard of critical care, safe anaesthesia and blood bank was far from extraordinary, especially in our hospital, these patients suffered.

There was hesitancy in doing any operative interference in these 'high-risk' patients. The idea was not to add surgical stress. It was years later when I had moved out of this hospital and saw lives saved by a judiciously timed caesarean section and a liberal use of blood products that I regretted our hesitancy and the unavailability of life-saving medicines and techniques. So many young lives could have been saved!

It was 15th August and that meant a full 24-hour emergency duty in the hospital—not something anyone would like to look forward to in a government hospital but life didn't always give you much choice. Dumping my carefully packed two-time meal in my duty room, I squared my shoulders and entered the war zone. I could feel the visible relief on the face of my colleague who was waiting to give me the mandatory 'over'.

'We had another one in the eclampsia room today. I just delivered her with forceps. The placenta is not yet out. She is sick,' my colleague warned me.

I understood what lay ahead. They were poor candidates for anaesthesia and any surgical intervention was the last option.

'The other three who delivered more than a day earlier are still on anticonvulsant drip and sedated. They are serious, too. You must remember to put down the half-hourly notes.'

I grimaced. An emergency duty also meant less staff. We were only three residents who were working that day.

Leaving the labour room, I started my rounds of the eclampsia room and the septic-labour room. Four in the eclampsia and two in the septic labour room were enough to strain any duty.

The rooms were as morbid as the diseases itself.

I finished checking the vitals and jotted down the notes of the first two beds, deliberately giving the third one time to deliver the placenta. But then it was already half an hour.

'Sister, please bring a tray.' I asked the nurse and hurried to the side of the patient. Without wasting any time, I put on my gloves and started taking out the placenta.

'It's not coming. I think it is adherent. It's so difficult delivering a patient on bed.' I complained as I twisted my back to examine her. It was definitely not a very comfortable position but these patients could not be shifted to the labour table.

As I struggled with the placenta, I felt there was an unusual stillness about the patient.

'Sister, call the doctor from labour room.' I shouted at the nurse.

She was unconscious. I stood up slowly and looked at her face. It was deathly pale and her eyes looked half open. Instinctively I took off my gloves and felt her pulse. My worst suspicion got confirmed. There was no pulse.

'Oh my god! I was delivering a dead patient.' I churned with nausea.

I had seen patients dying before but once again I felt the same raw pain and shock in my pits.

And I was the one responsible to report her death. I dashed to the labour room to call up our head of department.

'Ma'am, the patient in the eclampsia room is dead.' I spoke in a rush.

'It's okay. Take their signatures and hand over the body to the attendants.' For a change, her voice was soothing and lacked the usual authoritative tone. Maybe she could sense my anxiety.

'And Dr Varma is on call today. She is taking rounds. Talk to her if you need help,' she added. It dawned on me that I should have called Dr Varma first. In my haste I had forgotten the protocol and ended up calling the head of department directly.

I flushed. Thankfully she couldn't see me.

As soon as I entered the hospital, it was his shirt that I noticed first. It was stained bright red.

It was not a common sight to see a young and handsome guy in our labour room carrying a grim expression on his face and a woman in his arms and that too when it was well over midnight.

As my eyes travelled upwards, a muscle twitched at the corner of his face betraying his nervousness and I encountered a pair of eyes that looked back at me awkwardly.

The night had just begun for the hospital and for the couple too. The profusely bleeding, 23-year-old girl had been brought to the emergency by her boyfriend. The eyes that were looking back at me were those of the boyfriend. And my eyes were not the only ones staring at him. Many more pairs of eyes were taken in by the unfamiliar sight.

'So, why did you bring her here?' I asked.

'Well, actually, she was with me!' He replied.

'That can't be a reason enough.' I said.

I stared back and he flustered. Hopefully this didn't turn out to be a honeymoon couple or worse another medico-legal case. But, rather than speculating it was more important to attend to the one whose blood was plastered all over his shirt.

The thin girl lay flopped on the casualty bed. Her face averted, pulse and blood pressure both not recordable. Apparently precious amount of blood had been lost before she arrived. Some fast fluids later she at least started having some decently recordable blood pressure and a palpable pulse. The vagina was a bloody organ and sometimes it was bent upon proving its worth.

And she was still bleeding, so much so that her garments and sheets were all soaked. The boyfriend needed to donate blood since there was no one else in sight. It was equally pertinent to locate the cause and stop the bleeder from creating further havoc.

She was wheeled into the examination room and with some difficulty the offending blood vessel was identified along with an area of torn mucosa in the vagina. But it was located quite high up and she was understandably in a lot of distress. There was no way it was possible to repair it without anaesthesia. But anaesthesia or any surgery happened only after consent.

Her cheeks had regained some colour and she could at least speak.

'Madam, do I have to have a surgery?' She asked me.

I told her that she didn't have a choice.

'What will I tell my parents?' She looked worried.

It was always best to inform them and avoid getting dragged into any controversy later on.

'Can you please talk to my parents?' She pleaded.

'That's your job! Do they know about your boyfriend?' I asked.

'They do. But how do I tell them about this?' She looked worried.

I could only sympathise with her.

'Can I tell them it's because of PCOD?' She asked.

I turned surprised. How could a polycystic ovarian disease, a hormonal condition cause her to bleed like this?

'A PCOD to explain a tear in your vagina? That's illogical!'

'Please understand. You need to tell them that, else I cannot have a surgery. I just can't tell them the truth.' She was desperate.

'I can explain your situation to your parents but I shall not lie.' I refused to budge.

'That's fine, Doctor. But, in that case I will need to go home then,' she said.

This was ridiculous. She had been resuscitated with difficulty.

The 'honeymoon couples' were brought in similar situation but the legitimacy of it made things easier and the husband got away by merely some unkind and curious glances by the medical staff and a spoiled honeymoon. I looked at her thoughtfully.

'If it's an anaesthesia that disturbs you, we can try doing without that. I shall be quick but you will have to be very cooperative.' I offered the only solution.

She nodded eagerly.

Between behaving responsibly and that faint twitching that gave up his nervousness, the boyfriend tried unsuccessfully to behave like a 'grown-up man'. He signed the consent without much of a glance.

A 'night out' had got them more than they had bargained for.

As she was being wheeled inside the examination room, I tried to keep her busy.

'So your parents know about him?' I asked her.

'Yes, but if I tell my parents about "this", it is he who will be unnecessarily slammed for a guilt he has not actually committed alone,' she reasoned calmly.

I appreciated her sense of fairness.

If it was difficult to locate the bleeder, tie it and then stitch her torn vagina, then it was indeed brave of her to bear all the pain without any anaesthesia. As I finished off the marathon I remembered the restless boyfriend waiting outside. He deserved an explanation. Considering the preceding events that brought them here, I fumbled with the dos and the don'ts. I got interrupted just in time.

'I hope her PCOD will not bleed her like this again,' he asked.

I reeled. Seriously!

Considering the gravity of the situation I decided to ignore him.

'Well, we could just about manage to stitch her through. She is indeed a brave woman.'

'She'll be fine, Ma'am?'

'Of course.' I was at a loss to speak further.

'Why did it happen?' He asked me.

Well, that should have been my question. I was curious about that too.

'*You* can tell me that.' I said curtly.

'Well, I thought it was PCOD.' He looked a little uncomfortable.

At times I didn't understand if people were actually ignorant or if the circumstances made them stupid.

Whatever it was, most of the residents were having a gala time gushing over the handsome boyfriend.

'They look nice together and much in love.' Even the nurses drooled. It was indeed cute the way they kept holding their hands. And then in the middle of the night he went out to bring a pineapple pastry and chocolates for her. Of course she couldn't have it so soon.

Sameer's eyes grew thoughtful as I narrated the cute couple's story to him the next day. The cake and the chocolates! They always had that effect on girls. It made us so dreamy. I couldn't just stop praising the thoughtful gesture.

'I have an idea.' Sameer said brightly. I looked at him expectantly.

'Today when he goes to buy that cake and chocolate, ask him to bring some for you.' He said, tongue firmly in cheek.

If looks could kill, Sameer would have died that day.

'Seriously, after all that you did for them, without anaesthesia too, imagine!' He added.

I walked away as I would not have been responsible for my actions had I stayed back.

Though obstetrics kept us preoccupied for most of our post-graduation, it was gynaecology that kindled our interests. It was a cool branch, minus the unpredictability of obstetrics, the adrenaline rush of emergencies and also without the multitude of emotions attached with childbirth. It was more enjoyable and tested our surgical skills. The laparoscopic surgery was the upcoming trend and almost everyone dreamt of becoming a minimal-invasive surgeon. Gynaecology gave us a flair to experiment with new, innovative techniques.

Germany, with its laparoscopic training centre, was my secret destination.

Barring the operation theatres, the preoperative ward and the outdoor clinics were the places where we got exposed to the gynaecology patients. And we really looked forward to it.

But even as my love for surgery pushed me to hone my skills, not all patients were impressed by my zeal.

'Your patient is posted for surgery tomorrow.' I told the patient's husband.

'Sister, *surgery toh doctor sa'ab karenge na* (Sister, surgery would be done by the doctor only, isn't it)?' He folded his hands.

I fumed. Not again!

'I am not a sister!' I lashed back. It was another matter that even our teachers were called 'sister' by them.

'*Arrey* Madam, you are like my sister,' he apologised. He was not that stupid and realised his mistake.

'And who do you want to operate upon her?' I was still angry with him.

In simple words, *'Surgery toh doctor sa'ab hi karenge na'* meant that the surgeon had to be a male doctor.

Inspite of all my studies and training, I was reduced to a mere woman, at most a midwife incapable of doing surgeries because of my gender. I fumed inwardly but let it go.

I was waiting to go for my rounds, when I saw Dr Bali rushing down the stairs.

'You didn't advise the patient properly at the time of discharge. The one we operated on last Wednesday.' She was talking about a hysterectomy patient. And the advice was for abstinence. We had to strictly enforce 'no contact with husband' for at least six weeks post surgery.

'I must have.' I countered.

'You didn't.' She accused me. I had realised by now the futility of arguing with your teachers. I kept quiet.

'She landed up in the casualty just an hour back with profuse bleeding. Apparently they had sex last night and she's been bleeding since. Now they are denying it but we know better.' Dr Bali added.

Embarrassed by the disapproval in the eyes of the hospital people, the couple had taken to denial despite the initial admission of their 'guilt'.

'You should write in bold letters "ABSTINENCE" on the discharge summary.' Dr Bali thundered.

The problem was that they were illiterate. I could see Dr Bali was frustrated. We all got so involved and possessive about our surgeries.

The patient was taken back to the operation theatre and re-explored. And as always the fault was that of the resident.

'The patient that we were going to operate on Monday is refusing surgery.' I informed Dr Bali.

'Why?'

'She thinks it will adversely affect her relationship with her husband.'

'The couple is much concerned about their sexual life. They have been repeatedly asking the same question to almost everyone.' Even the staff was talking about them. 'I have counselled her so many times but she is adamant.'

'May be if they were much younger, you all would have been more understanding and sympathetic,' Dr Bali said with a touch of sarcasm. 'I will talk to them, later.' Dr Bali left after finishing the rounds.

I reached the outdoor clinic just in time and settled on the bench beside the final years and our house surgeons. As the senior most, I chose to see only the gynaecology patients.

'She' came and sat quietly on the stool next to me.

Something was bothering her. She kept shifting on her chair while her eyes kept darting to the door.

'Do you want your husband to come inside?' I asked.

'No, please. I would rather he stayed outside.' She said.

From where I sat I could see him clearly. An elderly man, he peered suspiciously through his thick-rimmed glasses. And so was this elderly woman who was fidgeting with a piece of paper lying on my table.

Government clinics hardly afforded any privacy given the rush they dealt with.

'You have children?' I asked her.

'Yes, two. They don't stay with us anymore.'

I looked at her enquiringly.

'Actually, my husband...' She hesitated, then stopped abruptly as if too embarrassed to continue.

'It's okay, please go ahead.' I urged her.

'I am no longer young and it is too difficult for me to be a proper wife to him in the true sense.'

'You still have to prove to him that you are a proper wife?' I couldn't help this.

'I hurt so much and my husband is getting frustrated. It's embarrassing but what should I do?' She sounded miserable. 'He has been pushing me to see a doctor but I...' Her voice trailed off. She looked around helplessly. The final-year students stared at her, not understanding her predicament.

The repeated attempts to be a 'proper wife' to her husband had left a trail of painful bruises on her now dry and constricted vagina. Aging had brought in some degenerative changes and she would need corrective surgery to restore her anatomy.

'But what do I tell my children?' She asked, innocently.

It was obvious she couldn't tell them the real reason.

'If it embarrasses you, you can choose not to tell anyone.' I suggested.

She nodded and left, promising to be back once they had discussed at home.

The next patient was nearly 70.

'Madam, I can feel something coming out.' She whispered shyly.

'For how long have you been feeling so?' I asked.

'May be for the last 15 years.' I was surprised.

She had a third-degree prolapsed uterus which meant almost the whole of the uterus was lying outside the vagina.

'Just how are you even sitting on the chair, forget emptying your bladder and bowel?' I dreaded imagining all that. 'Why didn't you come earlier? The results of the surgery would also have been better.' I asked her.

'I am sorry, Doctor. Fifteen years back my husband passed away and I had to single-handedly bring up my kids. My duties always took precedence.' She said.

There was something about these elderly women. Had they given up on life?

The next patient sat with shame written all over her face.

'I cannot control my urine. Earlier, it used to leak when I coughed but now it leaks even when I change sides or stand up.' She complained hesitantly.

She had been suffering from urinary incontinence for many years now.

'I am sick of the stench of urine. I have stopped going anywhere.'

Yet the hesitation in taking a medical opinion baffled me.

No wonder we had so many cancers these days, just because we failed to detect them at the pre-cancerous stage. Most of the symptoms were ignored under the garb of 'normal process of aging'. Even educated women did not get their PAP smear done.

Was it a feminine trait, being indifferent to their own health?

I was surprised to see Lata. She was just 28 and had been referred to the cancer hospital.

'Why did you come back?' I asked.

'We never went there, Ma'am. Our family decided to take local treatment.' The husband spoke guiltily.

All our efforts had gone down the drain for she had decided to go to some self-proclaimed 'doctor' who had guaranteed her a cure for her cancer. He used words, some herbs and blessings more than medicines to 'treat' Lata and some precious days later, the futility of it all sunk on her and she was forced to visit the hospital again.

She was now critical, in an advanced stage of cervical cancer (cervix though being the mouth of uterus, is a separate entity), with the tumour obstructing her urinary system as well.

'She needs treatment of her kidneys before any kind of therapy can be started for her cancer.' I said.

'I cannot do rounds of hospitals anymore, Ma'am.' Lata spoke breathlessly.

The sound of somebody sobbing disturbed the sudden silence in the clinic. It was her husband.

'How can I let her die?' He wailed.

'Why didn't you take her to the government cancer centre?' I asked.

'I wanted to but my family had blind faith on this man.'

'Who was this *doctor*?' I asked sarcastically.

'I don't know. She was taken there with a relative.' He was clearly evasive.

There was nothing unusual about this. These so-called doctors always enjoyed anonymity.

I sighed deeply.

'We tried to fix you up at the cancer centre. I can talk to my friend again.' I suggested.

'We went there too, Ma'am, but they do not have a kidney specialist. So they refused to take us up there.' He continued with his eyes downcast. 'Please keep her here, Ma'am.'

'Unfortunately, we don't have a dialysis unit.'

'Oh, we had got her card made at another hospital. Can I take her there?' He suddenly remembered.

The hospital he named had a good urology and dialysis unit. I fervently hoped they had a spare bed in the ICU too.

'That's a good idea. We can help you through our contacts there,' I said.

Precious time had been already wasted, and this was neither the time nor the place to speculate. Life, whatever was left, offered not many options and he had no other alternative but to shift.

Her face stared at me from the newspaper. Blood drained from my face. She had made it to the headlines.

'A 25-year-old doctor, working as house surgeon, committed suicide after she failed to qualify in the pre-PG entrance examination. Late night when her husband came back he found her lying unconscious in the room with white froth oozing from her mouth. She was rushed to a neighbouring hospital where she was declared dead. Her mother does not suspect any foul play.'

We live in a country where you don't qualify for a seat not because you were not competent enough but because there were not enough seats!

I was seized by sheer helplessness. How could she? Just a week back she had called up one of the residents.

'I was coming back from the village and our car met with an accident.' She said.

'Are you okay?' The resident was alarmed.

'Yeah, just minor bruises. But I won't be able to come for duty.'

'We will manage. Please take care.'

That was the day when the pre-PG exam results were declared. She had not made it. According to her husband she was depressed and kept herself locked in the bathroom. Two days later she had consumed some pesticides. She had bought them when they were returning from their village.

Things were not always like this with Kulwant. She was once a happy-go-lucky girl. After completing her MBBS she had moved to the United States. Somehow she couldn't find her way there. A little upset, she came back and joined our hospital as a non-PG house surgeon.

Her husband was her brother's friend who developed a fascination for her. She had known him for long and liked him. Rather than getting married to a stranger she accepted his proposal. They were soon married.

Her husband was a lawyer. It was after their marriage that the differences started surfacing. She was a modern girl from Delhi, and he belonged to a patriarchal, Haryana village. She was a doctor, he a struggling lawyer. She was fiercely independent, strongly opinionated; he came from a family where women were taught not to have an opinion. Soon their upbringing became apparent in their frequent clashes.

It didn't help when she was away from home most of the times. Her husband cribbed about her long duty hours and her frequent absenteeism from home. When she reached home she was usually too tired to work or even argue.

Once his parents had come to visit them. She tried her best to adjust her duties but couldn't as their program was made at the last moment. They didn't take it kindly and took it out on their son.

'What kind of daughter-in-law have you brought? She doesn't even bother to stay home for us.'

She entered the room just in time and heard them. When she tried to reason with her in-laws, her husband silenced her.

'Please do not raise your voice in front of my parents.'

Kulwant felt humiliated. Her husband was not a doctor and didn't understand the way the hospitals worked. The frequent fights were taking a toll in their relationship.

The problems at home affected her work. She became prone to frequent mistakes and was often reprimanded by her seniors. The long duty hours, stress at home and the lack of sleep added to her woes and she plunged into depression.

She had been working hard for the exams and was banking heavily on the results. This was the key to her happiness. But the results dashed all her hopes.

Her frail mental balance buckled. And one day the volcano erupted and she did the unbelievable.

There was a meeting called in her memory in the department.

'This is your house. But no exam is more important than your life. No matter what happens remember your parents didn't give birth to you for this.' For the first time I saw the professor get emotional.

Couple of years back a final-year postgraduate in our department had committed suicide just before her exams. She was not a very good worker and couldn't keep up with the rapid pace in which the hospitals moved. The frequent face-offs with her seniors were well known. Her death exposed everyone to massive press coverage and media slaughter. It was not only her family but almost everyone in the department who suffered. Her parents blamed the department for burning out the unfortunate girl.

New rules like mandatory weekly off days, not more than 48 hours a week duty amongst many other goodwill measures were framed—rules that were never followed but simply ate dust on the file papers of the department.

The department stayed in a sombre mood for sometime. Every little thing would remind us about her. But then in a hospital nothing stays around for long other than patients and their problems and soon everything was forgotten at the altar of work and duty. Life moved on, back on the same track.

My parents were getting restless. Whatever proposal they brought received the same reaction from me.

'I can't marry this one.' I cribbed.

'Just look at him!' I would groan at his picture.

'Our professions don't match. He would never understand!'

'I don't like his family. I can't live where he works.' I was quick to find faults.

My parents were getting frustrated. It's not that I was haughty or snooty, I could no longer think of marrying anyone else apart from Sameer. But unknown to me, my parents finally had a dream proposal. A doctor from AIIMS who was now a bureaucrat, he was posted in Delhi. And that was the last straw. Some I had refused for not being a doctor, others I refused because I always wanted to get married to an IAS officer after I gave up on my own dreams to become one. But since they had transferable jobs my career would suffer, hence I could no longer marry them either. This one gave me no respite and I floundered with my excuses. The boy's side was much more interested. They didn't even want any dowry.

'I have to discuss this with Sameer today.' I promised myself. It had not been easy working in the wards, preoccupied as I had been with all the turmoil going on.

'My parents are not ready to give up on this guy.' If Sameer was upset he didn't show.

'And I can't tell my parents about us. They will never agree.' I wailed. We belonged to different communities.

I felt guilty of breaking their trust. But then was it wrong to marry by your own choice?

'If you want to go ahead with this marriage, you can. I shall not hold any grudges.' Sameer said in a low tone.

I listened, shocked. Was that all? It really didn't matter to him? I pushed him away and drove my Scooty straight to the hostel. I didn't realise I was crying hard.

Meera was shocked to find me in her room. One look at my tear-ravaged face and she had a bad premonition.

'What's wrong?'

I kept on crying.

'If you don't tell me I shall call Sameer.' She knew about us. She was one of the few people with whom I had shared the changing dimension of our friendship.

'He says it's okay if I get married to someone else.' I managed to speak between hiccups.

'Oh come on! He must have said it to make things easier for you.' She tried to reassure me.

But I was beyond reasoning.

How dare he? Was it his refusal to commit that hurt me or was it his easy acceptance of the situation that piqued me? I wasn't sure but it demeaned everything between us.

I gradually regained composure and washed my face. Meera made a cup of tea for me.

'Now, go home. We will think about this later,' she said.

I was surprised to find Sameer waiting for me outside the hostel on his scooter.

'Well, if you have decided to be with me, then let's face this together,' he said.

I was too shocked to smile. I gaped at him.

'I hope you know what this means,' he added.

I nodded. No loud declarations of love, no fancy going down on the knees. Was this the closest it would get to my dream proposal?

I held his hand. I was suddenly engulfed by an intense joy and a sense of peace.

'We shall be together, isn't it?'

He smiled. 'It won't be easy. My family is going to be equally rigid.'

And that's how it was. The next few days saw my parents' bouts of anger. But somewhere between blaming themselves to blaming my friends to blaming me, they gradually came to terms with my decision. They had known Sameer for a long time. They liked him but the differences between our communities were too many. Moreover, my parents had been forced to give up their dreams, first of making me a bureaucrat, and now of having a son-in-law as a bureaucrat. But, they relented and became doting parents once again, this time to both of us.

Sameer's parents were steadfast in their refusal. They too played the part of angry and disappointed parents to the hilt. We had deprived them the privilege of selecting a bride for their son and along with it all the fanfare. But after the initial resistance they gave in. Children's happiness always took precedence for parents.

Our families had yet to accept each other but we had their approval.

Not all of my friends were amused, some were bewildered. And some were shocked!

'You didn't drop a hint,' Kavya said accusingly. 'My best friends!' She felt left out.

I flushed guiltily but could offer no explanation. Sighing, she wished me the best.

The medical superintendent, MS as we usually called him was a frequent visitor to the hospital. He would come for inspection daily in the morning. We called it 'the garden round' as inevitably that's where we found him. In the garden, talking to the gardener, surrounded by his coterie of employees! But, surely the hospital needed more than just the flowers.

'Our coolers do not work. The ward *bais* do not even fill them.' We cribbed. There was a strong union of workers and only the MS could control them.

'Ask the interns.' He snapped.

'Sir, that's insulting.' We gasped at the audacity.

'Don't you ask them to bring samosas. Is that insulting?' He gave back and all we could do was fret and fume.

Another time I barged into his office, one hot, searing afternoon. I was coming straight after getting into a heated argument with the labour room nurse in-charge. 'Sister, please leave some bed sheets and blankets for the duty room. They were not there in my last duty.' I was much irked by that and complained to the nurse.

'I do not have spare blankets or sheets for the doctors.' The sister was not in a very generous mood. 'Doctors don't have to sleep.'

'I refuse to do duty then.' I stared at her mutinously.

'That's your wish.' She stared back.

My intolerance was growing with the years that I had spent at par with the rising temperature outside. My patience snapped. I dived outside, took out my Scooty and drove straight to the MS's office.

'I refuse to any duty, Sir.' I was livid and almost in tears.

'*Arre,* sit down *beta*. First tell me what happened.' He said soothingly.

I narrated him the whole incident with the nurse. He called her up and spoke to her with authority.

'You can now go back.' He said firmly.

When I returned the sheets and the blankets were laid out in the duty room. Even the water cooler was full that day. Nothing came easy, you had to fight for everything. I smiled victoriously.

But the worst face-off was still not over.

One of our residents had been threatened by a patient's attendant outside the labour room. We had staged protest outside his office threatening to go on strike.

'Bring back the security guards.' There were only two left in the whole gynaecology department.

But the MS came up with a unique solution. He locked the gates outside the labour room casualty.

'Now no one can barge in. They will have to take a long way to reach here.' He claimed.

'This will also mean a longer way to reach our duty room.' We protested.

It was a lonely stretch at night, fraught with dangers but he refused to relent. The locks stayed along with our determination to not have them there. It made the whole duty cumbersome.

Few days later I was on duty along with Kavya when Sameer had dropped in to meet us. He was also busy in his studies and thesis these days. We barely met. The telephone was now our main medium of connect.

'This is getting so difficult.' Kavya sounded peeved.

'We must do something. It can't go on like this.' I added.

'Let's break the lock.' Sameer offered a simple solution.

The GRMC boasted of a lot of hot blood. Right from the MBBS days we were famous for our tiffs with the local administration. Our patience ran on a low threshold. We got embroiled with anyone who got in our way.

'We are from the medical college.' This got us around at most places. It was a small city unlike the metros and we flaunted our white aprons even outside the hospital.

Probably it was the raging Chambal river that flowed inside us and it simmered at the slightest provocation.

The plan was made. We just looked carefully around. The nurse was dozing inside. And the corridor was empty. It was now or never.

We geared up all our strength and there! We hit out.

The wooden plank with the frail lock came off rather easily. So much so for secure doors! Suddenly everyone was buoyant. The hurdle had been removed.

But it was not forgotten. The MS inspected it closely the next day. His clout surrounded him.

'Who could have done this?' The one behind him asked.

'I have a fair idea.' He looked obliquely.

Thankfully he didn't put the locks back. Things were back on the same track. No secure doors, no security guards. The threats and insecurities, now a thing of past! It was convenient to forget and move on. The world lived on false hopes and securities and so did we.

She entered the labour room just about the same time that I came inside. A patient of the professor's unit she was one of her 'private ward' patients. These 'white paper' patients, as we called them because they carried the white private clinic prescription, were VIP patients. They were treated with special care and caution. We needed to be in the good books of our teachers. With exams just around the corner, we couldn't afford to rub them the wrong way.

The consultant on call decided to see the patient before she went home in the afternoon.

'She is nicely dilated and has a good pelvis. She should progress well and deliver normally.' I was assured.

'Power, passage and the passenger, the three Ps are the tripod on which the success of a normal vaginal delivery depends.' Dr Batra would often reinforce in her characteristic style.

The passenger or the baby had to behave well and not get distressed.

The power, the pains or the uterine contractions had to be strong and drive the baby down and out.

The passage was the trickiest of all. A good passage could be narrow for a big-size baby and a narrow passage could be adequate for a small baby.

Meanwhile, the patient had been in labour for about four hours. I frowned.

'She is still five cm only. The head is also at -2 station, meaning it was still near the pelvic inlet.' I called up the consultant on call. The baby had not even entered the birth canal properly.

'Don't worry, she will deliver.' She sounded positive enough.

'Her pelvis appears to be a little small.' I tried to argue.

'Let's wait for two more hours.' She told me.

I couldn't take a caesarean without her consent.

The next two hours passed with difficulty but the baby's heartbeat was still good.

It was now 8 pm.

'Madam, she is now fully dilated and the head is also at zero station.' I informed my consultant on call. The head had moved down a little.

The patient was tired now. She had been labouring for long.

'There is some caput or swelling in the head now.' I couldn't help being worried. It could be an early sign of obstruction.

'I think you are just anxious. Caput can be present normally too.' The consultant said. She was right.

'Can't we take her up for caesarean?'

'We can't take her up just for a hunch.' She insisted.

The patient continued to labour and the head descended a little. I desperately wished for the consultant to be present. She generally came by late evening and then stayed the night.

'There is still time for her to come.' My house surgeon looked at the clock. These were the moments when I missed being a house surgeon. The carefree days when we were not the ones responsible.

The patient was now bearing down with all her might. Yet the head would descend with pain and then go back. There was no crowning. Crowning was a term assigned to a foetus that stayed at the outlet and didn't recede even after the pain was gone.

The consultant was still nowhere in sight.

'The heartbeat is slowing down.' The house surgeon alarmed me.

The baby was showing signs of distress. But with the head now so much down, caesarean was no longer a viable option. Still it needed to be taken out fast.

'*Push kar. Beta zor laga, zor laga.*' The nurse tried to motivate her.

The patient flopped back. Exhausted and drained out she had no will power left either.

I was being left with no option.

'I will have to apply forceps.' I asked the nurse to bring out the outlet forceps.

The swelling or the caput had increased taking away the chance of vacuum delivery.

We soon had the patient in position. Thankfully, the forceps could be applied easily. The right blade, then the left and then I locked them with a click. So far so good.

'Should I stand behind you?' The house surgeon asked me.

'To stop me from falling back?' I laughed. It lightened the atmosphere. 'I wouldn't need to apply that much force.' I was keeping my fingers crossed.

'I have already called the paediatrician.' She said.

With the next contraction, I pulled on the locked forceps. First down, then gradually up, delivering the head. I quickly unlocked the blades and delivered the rest of the baby.

I slumped my shoulder. Finally the baby was out!

But the baby was blue, limp and did not cry. The Apgar score dipped to 2. The paediatrician was trying to revive the baby. His hands pumped at the ambu bag to maintain the ventilation. The colour improved but it was still not crying.

'He'll be alright.' The paediatrician tried to reassure me but he failed. It was now five minutes post delivery. The colour was pink and the baby was moving the limbs but the cry was still feeble.

'We are shifting the baby to the nursery.' He had swaddled the baby.

'But how do I explain this?' I felt like crying myself.

The baby was being shifted to the nursery when the consultant on call arrived. She looked at the bundle in surprise. 'What happened?'

As I quickly briefed her the turn of events, she exclaimed, 'Why didn't you take her up for caesarean section?'

I had no answer to her question. I reeled with shock.

The next day, she went home but I still had a job left.

In the evening I stood outside the professor's clinic. She was busy with her patients. I peered inside. She had seen me.

The baby was still sick in the nursery and the professor had been visibly upset during the rounds.

'You can go.' The clinic attendant pointed inside.

I stood in the corner not knowing how to start. Thankfully, she was experienced enough to know what I had in my mind.

'Tell me.' She urged.

I narrated the whole sequence of events to her. She was going to be my internal. Why should I be punished for no fault of mine?

'Why didn't you call me?' She asked.

I kept quiet. Retrospectively everyone was wiser. Every labour was a trial of labour and you could never be sure till the end.

'It's okay. Go home but be careful in the future.' I bowed slightly and left.

This was a struggle for survival, not necessarily for the fittest but for the meanest too.

With the exams hanging like the sword of Damocles over our heads it was indeed getting difficult concentrating on the emergency duties. If studies kept you on your toes, duties ate away the precious time and made you prone to mishaps. After my 'near-miss' disaster most of my batchmates were cautious. But then fate is funny and mishaps have a habit of catching up with you unawares.

The patient belonged to a good socio-economic status.

'Hello, you are glowing.' I complimented her.

She laughed.

'Your baby looks big and healthy.' That made her happier.

'How big, Ma'am?' She asked.

'Probably more than 3 kg.' I said and she smiled.

The average baby weight in a government hospital that catered to poor, underfed patients was usually around 2.6 kg. 'It's safer to opt for a caesarean section.' I advised.

She refused saying, 'Let me at least try.' I had to relent.

To the delight of the patient, the labour progressed smoothly and the baby's head came out easily. But in the next few minutes the baby's shoulder got stuck.

'Pull the baby down.' Dr Bali had joined us in the labour room.

I pulled the baby, but the shoulders which have a bigger diameter than the head refused to budge.

'Sister, take her legs towards her abdomen and give me a pair of scissors.' She enlarged the episiotomy. The idea was to increase the space and dislodge the shoulder. The clock was ticking. The shoulder was still not free.

'Let's rotate the baby so that the front shoulder goes to the back.' Dr Bali said. The birth canal was oblique, placed in a way that put the shoulder behind at a lower level than the front. So when we took the front shoulder behind it went lower and got disimpacted.

'Put a finger and take out the limb from behind. Then rotate it so that the other one also comes at a lower level behind and then pull it out.' She rotated the shoulders and soon both the limbs were out.

'This was so damn tricky.' She heaved with the effort. When you are responsible for a life the stress can kill you too. When you fail your guilt never absolves you and people never forgive you.

'One more hair turned grey and one more artery in my heart got blocked today.' Dr Bali grinned.

But, all was not well and Dr Bali realised that soon.

The baby refused to move the stuck limb. It lay paralysed.

'In all probabilities she has suffered from Erb's paralysis.' Dr Bali said.

A rich plexus of nerves supplying the muscles of the arms got injured during the shoulder dystocia as we called it.

'It shall resolve soon, on its own.' The paediatrician was hopeful. The parents were aghast. A normal delivery was not always the best thing to happen, contrary to popular perception.

'No obstetrician wants to be stuck in this nightmarish position. It is difficult to predict. That's why doctors resort to caesarean section at the slightest hint of a big baby.' Dr Bali told us. 'Sometime back a shoulder got stuck. We tried everything, even tried to push the baby's head inside but couldn't.'

'Then?' I asked.

'The baby was dead. I had to decapitate and deliver.' Dr Bali said.

'I lack the expertise and the guts to do it ever. I will call you when am stuck there, Ma'am.' I said.

'Soon you will move out of this hospital and forget your poor teacher.' Dr Bali laughed affectionately.

'That day shall never come.' I reassured her.

We were getting sentimental. But yes, our days were now counted. This journey was coming to an end.

Surgical departments especially the ones which were busy like ours didn't have many lectures. The emphasis on teaching was negligible. Our emergencies were unpredictable and barring a few most lectures got postponed due to an emergency. We barely managed to get our seminars and case presentations through.

That day, we had a lecture on 'ureteric injuries'. But then like majority of times, Dr Mahajan got stuck in a difficult caesarean at the last moment. The lecture was called off. We couldn't hide our disappointment.

This was an important topic and we were looking forward to it.

Suddenly, we saw Dr Yadav coming from a distance. He was the urologist. A vaginoplasty surgery was going on. There were associated anomalies of the urinary tract too. Dr Yadav had been called to do the corrective surgery of the urinary tract.

'The beautiful girls of the gynaecology department!' He greeted us jovially.

'Good afternoon, Sir.' We greeted him back.

'But why the long faces?' He asked.

We told him about our bad luck. We all had come from home just for this lecture.

'If you girls have no problem, I would love to teach you.' He said.

We were overjoyed. A lecture on the ureter by the urologist was any day a boon.

Dr Yadav was an ardent teacher. He used anecdotes to explain the 'course of the ureter' and levels where it dangerously came close to our operating fields. The lecture was indeed very interesting. He made it simple too.

'Girls, though we don't mind coming any time you call us but the idea is to avoid the situation. And you all should be capable of first identifying your mistake and then rectifying it.' He said.

We were impressed.

'How was today's surgery, Sir?' I asked.

'The vaginoplasty? Your madam is an amazing surgeon.' He praised our professor. He too was an amazing one. I knew many medical students and even PGs who had a crush on this dynamic personality.

'Hey, let me share with you an interesting case that found its way to a urology journal.' We leaned forward, interested.

'This girl with a blind vagina was making love with a guy. They were actually indulging in fellatio, oral sex!' He grinned unabashed.

We were a little embarrassed but then we were grown-ups now. None of us chose to react.

'Suddenly, the girl was shot in her stomach.'

'Right in the middle of the act?' a student asked.

'Yes, but she didn't die. Her stomach got perforated. She was operated and thankfully survived.' Dr Yadav said. We sighed with relief for the unknown girl.

'A few months later she found out that she was pregnant!' He announced.

'How can that be? She had a blind vagina!' We found our voice.

'Exactly, I want you girls to tell me how!'

We fumbled for an answer but failed to come up with one.

'Let me tell you. The sperms had travelled to the stomach. So when the stomach got perforated by the gun shot, the sperms escaped into the abdominal cavity.' Dr Yadav explained.

We were listening spellbound.

'They were soon picked up by the tubes and the lucky sperm got fertilised.' His voice resonated with the thud on the desk.

'No, this is unbelievable!' We shook our heads.

'You girls think I made it up?' He sounded hurt. 'I will let you know about the journal.'

'With a blind vagina, how would she deliver?' The obstetrician inside us was roused.

'That's for you girls to decide.' He laughed. We couldn't help joining his banter.

The lecture was over. He had brought in that tinge of merriment to our otherwise dull and tense exam days.

It was our farewell party. Our immediate juniors and our teachers had chosen a delicious menu and the emotional speeches moved us to tears. A hundred memories were revoked. It was like we had not spent three years but a lifetime here. It was almost impossible to shrug it off and unbelievable to imagine a life outside the hospital.

'Your batch shall always stay in our memories. We wish you all success in your future endeavours. I hope you shall carry the legacy of KRH wherever you go.' Our professor said.

'Thank you, Ma'am.' We responded collectively.

All our teachers and senior staff members wished us good luck.

Post-graduation was also about relationships built and impressions created. If there was one thing that still troubled me, it was my bonding with the professor.

The few moments that I got to be personal with her were either uncomfortable or had got spoiled. And that distressed me now. The internals were your saviours and strength.

'You all must submit your thesis in the university before the last date. Remember, we won't be able to help you if you miss the date.' Our professor announced.

There, she had said that! You didn't qualify for the examination without the thesis!

Dr Batra was my guide. I had finished my thesis about six months back. For the last four months it was lying in the printing office. Those were the times when there were very few printers who worked on the computer. Dr Batra's students by default got their thesis printed from a printing office known to her.

Most of my batchmates had their theses ready, even those who had completed it much later. Moreover, mine was a little lengthy with complicated statistics and a huge master chart. And it was far from taking any shape. I was getting impatient.

'Stop looking so glum.' Dr Batra chided me as I stood with a long face in her office.

'I have spoken to Arun. He will start working soon. Don't worry.' She reassured me. Arun was the typist.

As I walked out with Sameer later, he said, 'Should we send somebody from the hostel to threaten her?'

'Stop it!' I laughed. You don't threaten your examiners.

The next few days tested my sanity as well as patience. There were last-minute goof ups.

'You just behave like my daughter. She too gets cranky unnecessarily.' Dr Batra tried to calm me down.

Was it unnecessary when only two days were left to submit the thesis and yours was nowhere complete? Things came to a boiling point when I got a call from Arun in the evening.

'Madam, your master chart can't fit into the book.' He informed me.

'What?' The thesis would be rejected without that.

'Why did you have such a huge master chart? Now we can just have another small booklet for that.' He said.

He should have told me this much earlier. I gritted my teeth. I was wasting precious time over these logistical things.

The next few hours saw me calling every technical help. Finally, one of my engineering friends offered a solution. It was reduced in size to fit the book. The thesis looked bulky and the printing got expensive, but at least it was complete in one piece. I was embarrassed by its size. But I had worked hard on it and didn't want to tamper it.

Finally, I got my thesis at 3 pm. It was the last day and the university closed at 5 pm.

Kavya had also not submitted hers in a show of solidarity. It was traditional to buy a pen set for your guides and get the thesis signed by that pen. We had ours ready. We rushed to Dr Batra's house. She chuckled at me while she signed our books.

'She reminds me so much of my daughter.' She said that again, this time to Kavya. She signed her thesis as well.

'Good luck to both of you.' We thanked her and left.

We then rushed to our professor's house. She was waiting for us.

Signing our theses, she wished us best of luck and said, 'Now rush off to the university. The office closes at 5 pm.' I realised that I was not the only one worried and it comforted me.

Sameer was waiting for us outside her home. We sped to the university.

Phew, we had managed. Both the theses got submitted barely 30 minutes before the office closed.

Sameer was looking oddly at our flushed faces.

Last-minute deadlines had their own thrills and adrenaline flow.

'You won't understand, Sameer.' I laughed at his odd expression. He had submitted his thesis a month back.

He laughed back. He too had been worried.

It was a day to celebrate. Even if we were the last yet it couldn't hamper the pride and a feeling of intense relief. That moment was ours, truly.

The exams were now just round the corner. The department was organising a conference. An erudite speaker from Baroda was invited to give a guest lecture.

'It is mandatory to attend this conference.' We were told. Initially I thought it was just to show the department in full strength and cribbed but then hints were dropped.

'This lecture on "Recurrent Abortions in Pregnancy" cannot be missed.' The professor gave us a long and meaningful look. We understood.

The speaker was charismatic and a wonderful orator. He brought fresh insights into the burning topic. We were mesmerised by his keen knowledge and spellbinding presentation.

'Is he going to be our external?' Kavya mused.

It was difficult to presume though rumours were rife.

But, very soon all presumptions and assumptions died as we were caught in the vortex of studies and examination.

Medical exams were a test of endurance. The never-ending courses not just tried your patience but your grit and the nerve to stretch yourself beyond limits.

Overcoming sleepless nights, throbbing headaches, burning throats and amidst parents who were too scared to even point out our weird behaviour and bizarre routine, yet forcing us to have sweet curd just before we left, we somehow found our way to the examination halls.

If there is a beginning there will be an end, and it was the same with the exams.

Theory papers ended in a daze. We didn't even bother to speculate whether they went off well or not. It was important that one battle had been fought and ended.

The other battle was soon to commence. However, in between there was no respite.

'You all report to the hospital tomorrow.' We were informed by Dr Batra.

So we were back to the same routine and it continued till a week before the practical exams started.

Somehow being in the hospitals till the very last days helped. It kept us engrossed. But once at home the pressure started showing. The impending practicals and the unknown externals started making us jittery.

'Why don't you go and see the patients in the wards? You will get an idea about the cases kept for examination.' Sameer advised me. It also helped being friends with your immediate juniors.

We got a fair idea of the cases admitted in the wards.

The day of the practical dawned and brought us back to the hospital wards. It was an eerie feeling. The same wards that had been a companion till now were going to test us. We were given small chits. On it were the names of the long cases that we were going to present.

Mine was pregnancy with diabetes, Kavya got pregnancy with high blood pressure and Rashmi got previous caesarean with twin pregnancy. There was a problem though. Kavya would have been happier with diabetes, Rashmi with high blood pressure and previous caesarean was my thesis topic. So, a silent agreement was reached. Soon we were at the bedside of our respective patients.

The examiners were smart but unrelenting. And, it didn't help when the candidates came out one after the other, depressed. I didn't asking anything from them. It was important to be focused on your case. For a change Kavya was happy when she came out. That infused some positivity in those who were waiting for their turn. She promised to wait outside with Sameer till I finished.

Finally, after a long wait, it was my turn.

I felt like a new pawn as I sat down in front of them. Soon they started baiting me.

'What is your case?'

'Previous caesarean with 37 weeks twin pregnancy.'

'How will you deliver her?'

'By caesarean section.'

'The impatient new generation!' The external from Alwar scoffed. How else would a twin with previous caesarean deliver?

The other external, the head of the department from AIIMS, looked kinder.

'So, tell me your steps.'

I started with the preparation of the skin and went about the steps of the caesarean section.

'I shall clean the skin with Savlon and Betadine.'

'Savlon?' The AIIMS professor looked surprised. 'We use only Betadine.'

'But here we use Savlon also.' Our professor intervened.

'By the way, why shouldn't you use Savlon, can you guess?' She was not easily put off.

'Because it's soap and can cause bad anaerobic infections.' Thankfully, I knew that.

They kept on pelting me with tricky questions. I kept on shielding myself with replies as much as possible.

Suddenly, the Alwar professor interrupted me.

'It's a previous caesarean and the bladder is adherent to the caesarean. Now, you suspect bladder injury. What will you do? Call the surgeon?' She asked sarcastically.

'No, Ma'am. I will repair it.'

'But how will you identify the injury?' She taunted me.

'I can see the Foley's catheter.'

'We don't always use that in every patient.'

We did but I kept quiet. The examiner should have the last word.

'The gush of urine.' I said.

She nodded.

'We can inflate the bladder with saline and check the leak.' I added. She nodded again. It was like checking a puncture!

'Do you notice something else, in the surrounding tissue?' She asked me.

'The pearly white lining of the bladder.' The AIIMS professor looked satisfied.

'Okay. We know that we have caused a rent. How do you plan to repair it?'

Urology system had a great fascination with me. While in the final year it had been all about kidney and the ureters, today it was all about the urinary bladder.

Soon, they had veered towards the suture material. Thankfully, I was prepared.

Another few minutes and I was out of the room. I felt free and at the same time a little drained and empty. Exams, they always brought upon weird feelings.

Still there were miles left to go. Tomorrow my battle would again commence. This time I would armour myself with gynaecology; instruments, contraceptives and specimens.

Sameer had come to receive me. The paediatric department was finished with their practical exams a day before and he was a free bird. I so envied him. He dropped me home.

We had a lecture by the external in the evening followed by dinner in the honour of our examiners. There was no question of absconding from there. Not even in name of exams the following day.

'Feminine forever,' the AIIMS professor talked about hormone replacement therapy which promised to revolutionise menopause care.

'Is that why she looks so smart?' We giggled. We were exhausted yet we still retained our sense of humour.

'The externals are not very happy. Most of the students goofed up.' Dr Varma informed me secretly. That was not good news at all.

'But she was happy with you and Kavya.' That boosted my spirits.

By the time I came back home it was already past ten. It had been a long, strenuous day and I tried hard to keep my eyes open and revise. But soon I was forced to give up and went to sleep.

The next day, both the examiners and the examinees woke up with fresh vigour and reached the front with new challenges.

'Today is our last official day together,' murmured Anuj. He had botched up his long case and was feeling very low. I felt sorry for him.

The examiners were not in a hurry. They took keen interest in every candidate and were thorough in their assessment.

While they pulled me up on prolapsed uterus, to Kavya it was fibroids that tested her patience.

Dysfunctional uterine bleeding as it was still called troubled almost everyone, and I remembered not to confuse progesterones with prostaglandins.

The day was coming to an end and we were getting a little impatient. It was around 4 pm when they wrapped up and predictably I was the last one. I fervently hoped that I made a dignified end to our two-day rendezvous.

As I walked out of the examiner's room, I was filled with a strange sense of elation. I sniffed and smelled freedom.

'Why are you sniffing like a canine?' Sameer laughed.

'We will take some time to become human again.' I felt dazed.

We stayed in the office for about two hours. Just in time I saw Dr Varma walk out of the office, tense.

'The Alwar madam is very strict. She has flunked many of you and is very unrelenting.' There was a collective cry from us.

'You and Kavya need not worry,' she whispered to me.

Now that was good news. I had never loved her more. I hugged her and touched her feet. She was embarrassed.

'Don't tell this to anyone.' She told me in a hushed tone.

'Cross my heart.' I grinned.

I sniffed again. I would take some more time to return to normalcy!

I looked around. The knowing corridors gazed back. They had watched me silently all these years, my fears, my anxieties, my awkwardness, my weaknesses, my goof-ups and my failures. They had accepted everything quietly and had watched my growing strengths with pride.

The darkness in the corridors was witness to Sameer and me waiting for each other, laughing with each other, matching our steps together and then crying for each other. From darting secret glances at each other to the lingering, first touch, the shadows had so lovingly engulfed everything. Would they miss us?

And would I miss this place? I looked around longingly at the hospital, the wards and the patients. My true teachers! They still looked bemused by all the attention, the abrupt change, the two-day-long drama and the unfamiliar cloak of etiquettes surrounding everyone.

I remembered the day of the medical entrance examination results. An image flashed in my mind—me and my sister holding the hands of my father, walking inside this campus. Had I finally reached my destination?

Sameer and Kavya were waiting for me. I walked out of the hospital, shrugging off the trailing shadow.

A warm gush of brightness enveloped me as I saw Sameer waving at me.

A journey was about to begin....

Acknowledgements

This is not only my book, nor are all the stories mine alone. This is a collection of stories, lived through the eyes of a medical student. To conceal the identity of real people, I have fictionalised some parts of these real-life experiences, which are set against the backdrop of my alma mater, GRMC Gwalior and the Kamla Raja Hospital.

When you write a book of such dimensions, you have a lot many people to thank. I was never alone in this journey so understandably the list gets longer.

I wouldn't be here if it were not for my parents Mrs Nirmala and Mr PK Sharan, who gave up on their own dreams so that I could pursue mine. They taught me the value of generosity, simplicity and the motto 'first deserve then desire'. It still drives me.

By now I have lived a life more with him than without him—my batchmate from my school days and later my husband, Dhiren Gupta has been steadfast in his support. He is the gush of 'Sameer' (air) who brought reprieve in my post-graduation days and together we have sailed through many complex situations. I still need to thank him for putting up to my 'no TV', 'no music' doctrines while I was writing, in the true spirit of a tolerant spouse. I hope he keeps that up for I shall hang on it for my future books too.

My children, Aryan and Manav give purpose to my life. I thank them for putting up with my absence and sometimes my writer's off moods.

My sister Rachna Varma has been my staunch supporter, even in my unconventional decisions. Right from my choice of career, my marriage to my recent writing stint, she has always been there to indulge my every whim and fancy. I thank her and her husband Ashwini for their contribution in my life.

My brother, Ankur Sharan needs a special mention for being my strength during my post-graduation days. Younger than me, he was forced to be old enough to pick me up whenever I got late from the hospital, despite his own studies. I thank him for prioritising my demands over his, always. I thank his wife Pallavi for carrying forward the tradition.

Dr JB Gupta, Savita Gupta, Ruchika Gupta and Manish Gupta; my in-laws who always had faith in my writing skills. I thank them for loving me and accepting me, despite all odds.

To Keerti, who has been my constant companion and a pillar of strength right from my school days, all through my college days, till now. I thank her for being there in all the highs and lows of my life.

To my friends and batchmates, Mamta, Rohit, Veeru, Yatendra, Sanju, Preeti, Ranjay, Neerja, the names are endless; you make up the gist of my undergraduate and post-graduate days. Thank you for adding fun and meaning to my life.

I thank GRMC, Gwalior and its attached hospital KRH for setting the stage of my life, my teachers of the department of Obstetrics and Gynaecology for putting up with the green horn and giving me the skills to stand on my own. I acknowledge their struggle in disciplining even the wayward medicos and evolving us into the present generation of dynamic and successful doctors. I bow in reverence to them.

I thank the nursing staff and the paramedical staff for teaching us beyond textbooks.

To my patients for placing their trust in our hands. They gave us the lessons of life and I acknowledge the contribution of each one of them. My friends and my colleagues at my work place, thank you for tolerating me and at times my weird behaviour.

To my publisher, Dipankar Mukherjee of Readomania for believing in my stories and cultivating a doctor into an author. I have yet to meet a more dynamic, more selfless publisher who steers his authors into limelight while quietly watching from backstage. Thank you for being my friend and guide, and also sharing my love for samosas!

My editor, Indrani Ganguly, braving medical problems at home, caught as she was between hope and anxiety, worked at the same time on my manuscript spread over medical trials and tribulations. I genuinely appreciate her for not once getting hassled by the medical jargons that took her to task. She has surprised me with her quick grasp of the difficult medical terminology. I thank her for the valuable inputs, the creative makeover that she has done to my book and above all for putting up with my jitters and irrational fears.

And in the end my readers, I look up to you with expectation. You have made it possible for me to share my experiences. I owe you my heartfelt gratitude. I have tried to put the technical words in a glossary for easy understanding. I thank you and shall forever appreciate your welcome comments and feedback.

You humble me for it is you who made me an author.

Tripti Sharan

2018

About the Author

A reader, writer, thinker and dreamer, Dr Tripti Sharan works as a senior consultant in BLK Super Speciality Hospital, New Delhi and is one of the most promising voices in the arena of contemporary English literature. With her dual role of a doctor-author and her distinctive style of writing in both prose and poetry, she occupies a significant place in the hearts of avid readers and literary enthusiasts.

She did her MBBS and MS (Obst & Gynae) from GRMC, Gwalior and thereafter moved to Delhi.

Having worked in both government and later private hospitals in Delhi, she's had a close brush with both the worlds. Obstetrics remains her first love and though it's a challenging branch with long and stressful working hours, it brings meaning and objectivity to her life.

Health, gender and social issues are close to her heart. Reaching out to people and inspiring them through her writings is her way of giving back something to the beautiful world that we live in. It has been the same zeal that took her to various platforms, sharing with people the myriad issues that plague women in India.

The difficulties in combating the prejudices and the social bigotry that exists in our society led her to penning her thoughts. Her book *The Chronicles of a Gynaecologist* published by Bloomsbury (2016), is a powerful women-centric book and is based on real-life incidences.

She recently came up with her volume of poems *Shadows of a Fading Twilight*. Earlier, her book on English poetry, *The Dewdrops...a Journey Begins*, was adjudged the best anthology in English poetry (2015) by '*Aagman*' literary group. She was also conferred the 'Global Youth Icon Award 2018' by the Writers Capital Foundation for her work in literature and in serving humanity.

Apart from writing for various forums like *The Better India*, *Different Truths* and *NDTV everylifecounts*, where she tries to showcase the myriad issues that plague women, she is also an active blogger with webzines and contributes stories and poems to anthologies and publications.

An ardent swimmer and a fitness freak, she's married to a paediatric intensivist, and has two boys. When she is neither writing nor practicing in the hospital, she listens to music, reads books, or spends some time idling with her family.

She can be reached at:

Email: triptisharan2003@yahoo.co.in

Facebook: https://www.facebook.com/tripti.sharan

Twitter: https://twitter.com/triptisharan200

Linkedin: https://www.linkedin.com/in/tripti-sharan-2630731/

Blog: https://musingzz.wordpress.com/

Glossary

Ambu bag	A handheld device to provide ventilation to patients not breathing at all or not breathing adequately
Amenorrhea	An absence of menstruation
Apgar score	A scoring system to measure the condition of a newborn. It is obtained by adding points (2, 1 or 0) for the heart rate, respiratory efforts, muscle tone, colour of skin, response to stimulation. A perfect Apgar score is 10
Blind vagina	A short vagina which is not connected with the uterus
Caprolalia	The involuntary and repetitive use of obscene language, as a symptom of mental illness or brain disease
Chait	Hindi month, generally around March and April
Crowning	A stage in labour when the foetal head stays at the vaginal outlet, doesn't recede back even after the contraction has passed off
Dai	Traditionally, village women who act as midwives
DIC	(Disseminated Intravascular Coagulation) A serious bleeding disorder triggered by widespread consumption of clotting factors leading to its deficiency and thereafter bleeding
Eclampsia	A complication in pregnancy when a woman suffering from high blood pressure in pregnancy throws up convulsions

Ectopic pregnancy	A pregnancy that is not at its normal position inside the uterus but outside the uterus, most commonly in the tubes
EDTA	A chemical used in blood collecting vials to prevent clotting of blood
Embolism	When a small clot of blood, tumour or air travels in the blood circulation to eventually block the artery
Episiotomy	An incision/nick given on the perineum to facilitate vaginal delivery
Foetus	The baby inside the uterus is called foetus
Foley's catheter	A catheter inserted in the urinary bladder to drain urine
Gravida	The total number of conceptions a woman has had, regardless of outcome
GRMC	Gajra Raja Medical College, Gwalior
Gynaecology	A branch of medical science that deals with the diseases of the female genital tract
Hydrocele	A swelling of the scrotum because of fluid collection around the testicles
Inguinal lymph nodes	The glands present in the groin that may enlarge in response to any infection or cancer
IV	Intravenous
IUCD	Intra uterine contraceptive device like Copper-T
KRH	Kamla Raja Hospital
Laparotomy	A surgery that involves opening of the abdominal cavity
MLC	Medico-legal Certificate

MS	Medical Superintendent
Nirodh	A brand of condom
Obstetrics	A branch of medical science that deals with pregnancy, childbirth and the post-partum period
Omentum	A sheet of fatty tissue guarding the bowel, stomach and other abdominal organs
Para	The number of births a woman has had after 20 weeks of pregnancy
Pearl Index	It is used to measure the effectiveness of a birth control method
Pelvic cavity	This refers to the bony birth canal
Peritoneum	The inner most lining of the abdominal wall
Placenta Previa	When the placenta is at an abnormal position, in the lower body of the uterus instead of the upper part, increasing the risk of bleeding and caesarean section
POCs	Products of conception, usually refers to retained tissue after an abortion
Post partum	The period after delivery
Rectus sheath	A tough sheath that lies just above the rectus muscle, in the abdominal wall
RMO	Resident Medical Officer
RSO	Resident Surgical Officer
Shock	A state of circulatory failure with no recordable pulse and BP
Vaginoplasty	A surgery done to create or reconstruct the vagina
Venflon	A plastic tube that is inserted in the veins to give fluids and injections.